Please return/renew this item by the last date shown. Books may also be renewed by phone or internet.

💻 www3.rbwm.gov.uk/libraries

☎ 01628 796969 (library hours)

☎ 0303 123 0035 (24 hours)

D0228646

PRAISE FOR DAVE RUBIN

"Dave Rubin's willingness to have tough conversations with those with whom he disagrees has made him a political force—and a target. This book shows why."   —Ben Shapiro, author of *The Right Side of History*

"Dave Rubin is bridging America's great divide. He reminds us that, while we may not always agree with the 'other,' we need to LISTEN to them. Rubin has mastered the vital skills of listening and of asking questions that do not serve an ideological agenda."

—Eckhart Tolle, author of *The Power of Now* and *A New Earth*

"Dave Rubin has been years ahead of the mainstream media, for years."

—Peter Thiel, entrepreneur and investor, author of *Zero to One*

"Dave Rubin is one of the bravest, smartest people I know, as well as a tremendous television presence."

—Tucker Carlson, Fox News host and author of *Ship of Fools*

"Dave Rubin is one of a kind. A truly great interviewer. Bright, curious, and funny."   —Larry King, host of *The Larry King Show*

"Dave Rubin's genuine curiosity and willingness to seriously consider opinions across the political spectrum have rightly made *The Rubin Report* a necessary corrective to modern journalism. *Don't Burn This Book* charts his personal and political transformation from predictable progressive to independent and informed thinker in a manner that his readers should find topical, engaging, personable, and, above all, reassuring."

—Dr. Jordan B. Peterson, author of *12 Rules for Life* and *Maps of Meaning*

DON'T
BURN
THIS
BOOK

CONSTABLE

DON'T BURN THIS BOOK

Thinking for Yourself in
an Age of Unreason

DAVE RUBIN

CONSTABLE

CONSTABLE

First published in the United States of America in 2020 by Sentinel,
an imprint of Penguin Random House LLC
This edition published in Great Britain in 2020 by Constable

1 3 5 7 9 10 8 6 4 2

A CIP catalogue record for this book
is available from the British Library.

ISBN: 978-1-47213-452-3 (hardback)
ISBN: 978-1-47213-451-6 (trade paperback)

Book design by Ellen Cipriano
Printed and bound in Great Britain by Clays Ltd, Elcograf S.p.A.

Papers used by Constable are from well-managed forests
and other responsible sources.

MIX
Paper from
responsible sources
FSC
www.fsc.org   FSC® C104740

Constable
An imprint of
Little, Brown Book Group
Carmelite House
50 Victoria Embankment
London EC4Y 0DZ

An Hachette UK Company
www.hachette.co.uk

www.littlebrown.co.uk

For Ben Affleck

CONTENTS

DON'T
BURN
THIS
BOOK

1

It's Time to Come Out

THE ORIGINAL TITLE of this book was *Why I Left the Left*.

For many months, the master plan was to give a definitive account of my political evolution. But, as soon as I cashed the publisher's advance check, I decided that wasn't the book I wanted to write.

You don't need me to go on for 250 pages about how the left has completely lost its mind. You already know this—at least on an intellectual level—and you can probably appreciate why I, a former lifelong lefty, have changed my allegiance.

This is because (as if I haven't said it on *The Rubin Report* enough already!) the left is now regressive, not progressive.

What was once the side of free speech and tolerance—the one that said, "I may disagree with what you say, but I will fight to the death for your right to say it"—now bans speakers from college campuses, "cancels" people if they aren't up to date on the latest genders, and forces Christians to violate their conscience.

They also alienate sensible grown-ups who dislike high taxes, oppose open borders, enjoy the free market, and harbor a healthy distrust of socialism. They're equally unwelcoming for sane, decent people who happen to be fiscally conservative, classically liberal, libertarian, or—dare I say it—the worst thing of all: straight, white, and male.

Rather than being all-inclusive and fair, the left is now authoritarian and puritanical. It has replaced the battle of ideas with a battle of feelings, while trading honesty with outrage.

So, instead of retracing why I left the left, what you need is a book about how to leave the left—and where to go next. You need a path forward—a road map of how to get there.

And even if you've left the left already, or never were part of the left in the first place, this book will help you understand our crazy political climate.

No matter what brought you to this book, I'm guessing you're trapped in a political purgatory with "tolerant" progressives who are holding you hostage. Perhaps you still cling to a few old-school left-wing principles but deviate from the party line on a few others—which is completely reasonable, yet you spend a lot of time self-censoring for fear of saying something slightly "un-woke" and unleashing the mob.

If so, don't worry. You're not alone. Over the past few years, I've received countless emails from various people who bite their tongues and keep their opinions secret every single day.

If you're in denial about whether this applies to you, ask yourself: Do you ever find yourself seeking out certain sections of the bookstore when you're alone? Do you crack self-hating jokes to double-bluff your way through the day? Or do you dither over what's diplomatic for your Facebook feed?

Do you secretly watch Fox News with your finger on the back button in case somebody enters the room? Do you methodically clear your browser history to erase all evidence of PragerU videos? Do you hide your subscription to Ben Shapiro's podcast? Or worry that your kid brother will catch you laughing at a Stephen Crowder video?

Maybe you don't want your friends knowing that you read books by Jordan Peterson or newspaper columns by Bret Stephens? Or you're ashamed of watching YouTube's *The Rubin Report*, which is hosted by the very scary (but quite dapper) Dave Rubin?

If the answer to any of these questions is yes, then I'm afraid you're living in fear of the woke machine. You're politically closeted, and it's time to come out. This book will show you how.

Trust me, I know how it feels to deny the truth and to hide from the world all too well. I was a closeted gay man—without a single person I felt like I could be honest with—for twenty-five years, and it nearly broke me.

Every day that I denied my reality, I became increasingly lonely and depressed.

It got so bad that my doctor put me on a powerful antidepressant called Celexa and told me to start seeing a shrink. Unfortunately, the medication didn't work and I never really connected with my therapist. She did, however, make one astute observation: she said I had the perfect blend of Catholic and Jewish guilt—the first is giving a blow job and feeling bad over it, while the latter is giving a blow job and worrying what your mother will think.

Without medication or therapy, I found other ways to cope with my depression. I began doing stand-up comedy six nights a week, which was an easy way to avoid the dating scene. But when I moved to Manhattan after college in 2001, my shame reached its tipping point and I'd developed a habit of downing bottles of cheap red wine alone in my apartment. To top it off, I also turned into a pothead.

One day in early September, I was walking through the Upper East Side when I began to hallucinate. I thought the buildings on both sides of the street were shaking, swaying from side to side. It was like a scene from Christopher Nolan's psychological sci-fi movie *Inception*, or Woody Allen's *Deconstructing Harry*, in which Robin Williams is forever out of focus from the rest of the cast.

This was the moment I knew I had to get a grip on reality. I was literally self-medicating to the point of delusion and it scared me straight (pun intended).

So, later that day, I reached out to my good friend Mike, who was one of the first openly gay comics in the city. We knew each other from the stand-up circuit and often went for drinks. He had no idea what was coming that random Monday evening, but at the end of the night—as we parted ways at the Times Square subway station around 12:30 a.m.—I came out for the very first time.

Instantly, I felt a massive wave of relief crashing over me. The world seemed so much bigger, brighter, and bountiful as I walked home—and, contrary to the warnings of televangelist Pat Robertson, I hadn't been struck by lightning.

Instead, I felt buoyed by a huge rush of adrenaline. As I climbed into bed, the future seemed truly exciting. That night I slept better than I had in years.

But the next morning I was jolted awake by a panicked phone call from my dad. He was clearly distressed, so I thought somebody had died—until he told me that he'd just seen a plane hit the World Trade Center's South Tower. Apparently, a second plane had hit the North Tower just eighteen minutes earlier. He could literally see the smoldering buildings from his office in the Garment District of Midtown Manhattan.

Shocked, I turned on the TV to CNN and there it was. America was under attack. When I walked outside, I could taste the black, acrid smoke against the roar of police sirens. Hundreds of dazed and confused people had brought First Avenue to a standstill.

Like them, I felt totally stunned by the worst terrorist attack on U.S. soil, but I also felt a strange sense of guilt about it all. It sounds crazy and deeply self-absorbed to admit now, but as this ungodly horror was unfolding, I honestly thought it had something to do with my coming out. I'd released this awful secret into the world, and now the world had struck back.

I was so twisted by the closet's solitary existence that I genuinely believed 9/11 was a consequence of my coming out just a few hours earlier. That's how fucking insane the closet makes you. It's a depressing, solitary place where there's only room for one. There's no light, no air, and no comfort. Just you and your private, dysfunctional thoughts stuck in a constant feedback loop from hell. It's a danger zone for your happiness, your relationships, and ultimately, your identity, which is why it must be vacated early on.

Otherwise, it produces a cycle of shame, deceit, and self-loathing that, once started, is hard to stop. You'll morph into a proficient liar, your friends and relatives will never get to know the real you, and perhaps most tragic of all, you'll never truly know yourself.

As if that isn't enough, staying closeted also changes your relationship with reality. That's because every time you're inauthentic with the universe, you're disrupting your experience of it. This

5

sends truth into a state of flux, distorting everything around you. It's like an endless, bad trip.

Conversely, the more you operate truthfully, the more reality remains stable and order manifests in your life.

Despite all of this, the proverbial closet has never been busier. Good, decent people just like you are lining up to lock themselves away from the real world for a whole host of reasons. Some are motivated by self-loathing, while others fear rejection and even professional suicide.

Each individual story is different, but they all share the same common through line: the abject fear of being themselves in today's modern world.

Fortunately, in the months that followed September 11, 2001, I witnessed courage in others that inspired me to up my game. As a result, I forced myself to be more honest with more people, more often, even if it pushed me out of my comfort zone.

Eventually, I was living my truth in real time, every single day, until it became my new normal. I was finally being myself.

Now, twenty years later, my life is exponentially better as a result of this—professionally, personally, and psychologically. Sure, if I'd done it sooner, I could've saved myself a whole bunch of pain and heartache along the way, but hey, hindsight is 20/20, right?

This lesson was incredibly useful when I found myself hiding in the closet yet again: this time, for my political beliefs.

If you've been watching *The Rubin Report*, you probably know that my intellectual journey from progressive to rediscovering what it means to be truly liberal has been a long one. But it's also been facilitated by some of the world's greatest contemporary thinkers, including Jordan Peterson, Sam Harris, Ben Shapiro, Thomas

Sowell, Dennis Prager, Bret Weinstein, Ayaan Hirsi Ali, Christina Hoff Sommers, and Peter Thiel.

They too came out of the political closet and helped me to see that tribalism is dead, and that diversity of thought is far more important than diversity for its own sake. Now, having gone through the coming out process twice, I'm imparting my wisdom to you.

After you read this book, you'll have no excuses left. You won't be able to hide anymore.

Part biography, part blueprint for a future that's firmly rooted in the individual rather than the collective, this book details the current madness of the left and, more important, gives you the intellectual tools to figure out who you really are—and with whom you will ally—in these crazy, confusing times. It's a road map back to sane, balanced thinking that's liberal in the historical sense, regardless of your political persuasion.

This book is your ten-step guide for political authenticity. In it, you'll learn how to:

- **Embrace your wake-up call:** It's the catalyst that brought you to these pages in the first place.
- **Think freely or die:** You'll get a much-needed crash course in classically liberal principles that stand the test of time. This is not a policy subscription for every issue of the day. It's a guidebook to the underlying principles that will help you navigate our political landscape. Liberalism, not leftism, is the best way of thinking that leaves room to agree to disagree, to change your mind as you learn new information, and to be tolerant of others—while remaining intolerant of intolerance. From here, you'll make decisions that

are best for you, which in turn will be best for the people and community around you.

- **Stop worrying about whether you're a Nazi:** If you decide to embark on this intellectual journey, a member of the woke mob will undoubtedly accuse you of being a Nazi. In this chapter, you'll acknowledge the (ridiculously) obvious truth that you are not, in fact, a Nazi. By truly owning this knowledge, you'll free yourself from the number one weapon that authoritarians have in their arsenal: shaming. Once you let go of this undeserved guilt, you'll remove the power from this loaded word by stopping such accusations to control the way you think. Sure, you know that real racists and bigots exist, but that doesn't make you one of them. Obviously.

- **Check your facts, not your privilege:** Perhaps most important, you'll also arm yourself with some facts that will enable you to combat some of the most pervasive political myths of our time, from the wage gap to climate change. All too often we go into conversations, arguments, and debates without proper information at hand. Instead, we rely on some general sense of what we believe. You'll also learn how to have more productive political dialogue, making Thanksgiving dinner with your loud, opinionated uncle a bit more bearable.

- **Never, ever surrender to the mob:** Once you have the facts, it'll also be much easier to resist the outrage mob. Currently, one of the key tricks the mob uses is to keep you second-guessing yourself, something that's quite easy to do when you don't know what you're talking about in the first place. If you are telling the truth, though, and keeping your cool, you can not only stand up to the mob but also stare them down. At times it'll seem like your entire life is about to become undone, but the secret of the mob is that it is always looking for new prey. It's a little dog with a loud bark, and eventually, if you don't give it what it wants—in this case your apology or surrender—it'll quickly get bored and move on to its next target. In the midst of this you will find out who your friends are, either through their support or their attacks, but you will come out stronger. Know that and don't be afraid.

- **Stop hating America, the West, and straight white men:** One of the motivations you'll have to stand up against the mob is that you'll love your country, the straight white men within it, and Western values in general. In fact, you'll know that America isn't perfect, nor could any nation ever be, but that she has granted more people more freedoms than any other country in the history of the world. You'll also know that straight white men aren't evil (it's actually racist and sexist to believe so) and that Western values rooted in individual rights are the cornerstones of free societies. Defend them proudly!

- **Learn how to spot fake news:** So much of this hatred comes from our deeply corrupt mainstream media. Activists pretending to be journalists have helped spread fake news more than Donald Trump ever could do on his own, so we'll look at how to spot the lies. You'll learn that the blue-check Twitterati at *Vox, BuzzFeed,* and *HuffPo* release ideologically driven articles presented as legitimate journalism.

You'll no longer believe that just because the staff at *The New York Times* and CNN once did their jobs they also do it now. Instead, you will become a discerning consumer of news, a person who challenges their beliefs and understands that if a story fits a narrative too well, then it's probably just propaganda. This partisan activism is partly what has led to the hysterical nature of cable news and clickbait culture that we see today. It's not really important who knows more, or who has the truth on their side, it's about who feels the most righteous. This can be fun and it can go viral, but knowing facts and fighting for the truth are far more important and eternal. Return to these pages when need be.

- **Find a mentor:** In this chapter, you'll learn why a smart, complementary mentor is the ideal as you cultivate your new future. You'll also hear the lessons I was taught by my friend and mentor, Jordan Peterson—the psychology professor and global phenomenon. He's had an indelible effect on the person I am today, and I had the honor of touring alongside him for two years. He helped me become a better person, and I hope that sharing my journey will give you a little something extra to ponder too.

- **Move on with your life:** You'll understand how to pack all of this stuff away and go live your life away from endless introspection, self-obsession, and navel-gazing. Sure, it's important to be switched on, but it's unhealthy if you can't switch off. Chapter 10 gives you express written consent to stop politicizing everything in your life. Trust me, this is a game changer.

Don't Burn This Book may not usher in world peace, balance the national debt, or improve your sex life, but while those are worthy pursuits, that wasn't my goal. Instead, I want to champion the values that keep people safe, sane, and free.

The reason? These shared values are under threat. We currently live in a time when people from the world's freest societies are afraid to speak up for fear of an outrage-fueled mob. Sure, these people can be intimidating, but if they haven't stopped me, then they shouldn't stop you. In fact, the world desperately needs people like you—unafraid of the truth and brave enough to stand up for it—no matter the consequences.

All right, now let's get to it, you racist, sexist, homophobes . . .

2

Embrace Your Wake-Up Call

THEY SAY THE first step to recovery is admitting there's a problem.

This, therapists believe, is crucial, because denial ain't just a river in Egypt. It's something that keeps people trapped in a cycle of dysfunction—with no motivation to change, ever.

Unfortunately, breaking through years of self-deception can be tough. The prospect of so much heavy lifting often puts people off, causing them to double-down into themselves, rather than to push through to the other side.

But by virtue of the fact you're here now, we've already established this isn't you.

Usually, at this point in the recovery process—when someone first acknowledges his or her issues and tries to unpack them—programs such as Alcoholics Anonymous will insist that the person stop drinking.

This is different. I want you to get "sober" through compulsive *thinking*.

That's right, people, I want you to walk into a bar and order yourselves a full-bodied opinion. I want you to get absolutely wasted on facts until 3:00 a.m., and then, when you're just about ready to pass out, I want you to get another large glass of reality and chug it.

I then want you to have intellectual binges that are so wild you go missing for days, eventually waking up on a stranger's sofa, hung-over on reality.

OK, this technically makes me your enabler, but that's cool because—spoiler alert!—you're not the problem here. It's what you're not doing.

Chances are you've seen all the red flags throughout the past few years, but failed to react appropriately out of loyalty, optimism, and a fear that if addressed, the fallout could be toxic. You're worried about losing friends, the prospect of awkward family dinners, and what perfect strangers might say to you on Facebook. But that fear has to end and it has to end now.

See, there is no reason to believe that you will ever be braver than you are right now. In fact, chances are you'll become less brave as time goes on. And if you miss the boat, there's a good chance you'll end up stranded.

So, to help you achieve what shrinks call "the breakthrough," consider this book the literary equivalent of a hazmat suit. Except, rather than handle radioactive chemicals, you'll face a truth that's only hazardous to your health if you continue to ignore this: *the left is no longer liberal.*

Once upon a time, the left truly was liberal. Liberals used to champion the rights of women, black people, and gays. They fought for all marginalized groups to be equal under the law.

This was authentic liberalism based on individual rights and it was a damn good thing.

Unfortunately, this is no longer the case.

Trust me, this is not some random assumption I've pulled out of thin air. It's a sober conclusion I've reluctantly reached after years of watching my old "team" transform into a baying mob of hysterical puritans—a feral gang that sows division through identity politics and encourages societal tribes to rank themselves in a pecking order of "oppression."

The left's vision is a new social order that despises our hard-fought freedoms (eroding the First Amendment in favor of hate-speech laws), promotes socialism (through the redistribution of wealth), and denies scientific fact in order to weaponize the power of feelings (by asserting that there are more than two genders, for example).

Worse still, they implement all of these things with brute force: violence, censorship, character assassination, smear campaigns, doxing, trolling, deplatforming, and online witch hunts. Tricks that are deliberately designed to leave people down and out. Ideally, jobless and without the resources to push back.

If you see no problem with all of this, or even condone it as part of a greater "good," then we have some serious work to do. You've got Stockholm Syndrome and need urgent intervention.

But if you want a world where people are judged equally by their actions, rather than by their immutable characteristics, such as race, gender, or sexuality, then—woohoo!—you're already on the right track. You're awake, rather than "woke."

Getting to this point isn't easy. In fact, it usually takes years of hard labor because our factory settings—everything the system teaches us to believe—are programmed into us from a young age.

These include a range of 2-D arguments that simplify life and position our starting point on the left, such as Democrats = good, Republicans = bad, progressives = humane, conservatives = merciless, socialists = generous, and capitalists = greedy, etc.

These presumptions are obviously fallacies, but they're easily swallowed by the idealistic and impressionable youth. The message is even more appealing when it's constantly reinforced through academia, the media, and celebrity, which make it look cool and credible.

Years of conditioning take hold before anyone even starts to question whether Barbra Streisand and Cher are wrong about foreign policy, immigration, and free speech—and by then, you're in too deep to simply walk away. It's like a controlling relationship. Or the hot girl who catfishes on Instagram. Underneath the filter, it's a different story . . .

My personal wake-up call happened in three parts.

It first began in 2013, when I relocated from New York City to Los Angeles, California, in order to join *The Young Turks* TV network. As a registered Democrat who had only voted for Democrats, including Barack Obama twice, this was a dream come true for me. Finally, I was in the "good" fight with my fellow liberals.

Unfortunately, the honeymoon period wore off within the first year after what I imagined *The Young Turks* to be didn't match the depressing reality. My colleagues positioned themselves as moral guardians of the new media. It quickly became clear to me that they were just pushing propaganda by selectively editing stories to drum up click-bait headlines, without ever considering counternarratives or challenges to their agenda. In essence, they designed the first model of the dangerous outrage machine that produces what we have come to call fake news. In the beginning I'd dismiss this and always try to push the narrative back into the center while discussing whatever political dramas were big at the time, but every debate seemed to end with somebody, somewhere, being called a bigot—just for having a different opinion.

Simply put, no matter what the conversation was about, there was always a smear on hand to shame someone into silence.

At first, I believed these accusations—why wouldn't I? There's no smoke without fire, right? Wrong. This became abundantly clear to me when the network's main host, Cenk Uygur, launched a scathing attack on conservative commentator David Webb.

In a heated segment about racism, Uygur described Webb—who's black but questions the narrative that America is a white-supremacist nation—as an "Uncle Tom of the conservative movement," adding he'd betrayed his African American roots in order to succeed in "white society."

"David, I hate to tell you, but you're still black!" he spat to the camera one day. "You can be their bitch all day long [but if anything ever happens to you, Fox News will defend your white shooter]."

Foaming at the mouth and wide-eyed, Uygur then invited his co-hosts to join the pile-on. They needed little encouragement to smear Webb as "Tucker [Carlson's] bitch" and even implied he'd "sold out" his own children to get a media career.

"[He's] Fox News' very own mouthpiece for antiblack sentiments," members of the crew said. "It's not an easy statement for us to make, unless it's completely earned."

Little did they know that I knew better—Webb was actually an old friend of mine and we went back many years. We'd previously worked together at SiriusXM radio, when I'd appear on his show to debate hot topics from a liberal standpoint. Although the subject matter was sometimes contentious, we always kept it civil and soon became buddies. (In fact, I can tell you two things for sure about Webb's character: first, he can knock back bourbons without flinching, and second, he's the real deal and truly believes what he says. And not only does he say what he believes, but he can also support his beliefs with facts.)

Because I knew Webb firsthand, alarm bells began ringing in my head. Here was a good man being lambasted as a fraud by "tolerant" progressives.

I couldn't help but wonder: Why would color-blind progressives be slamming Webb on his ethnicity? Would they have treated him this way if he were white? Weren't we supposed to be the good guys, the non-racists?

Quickly, my co-host's motivation became clear to me: It was character assassination in the name of self-protection. They wanted to kill Webb's credibility before his opinions could slay their entire worldview. To them, he was just an inconvenient black dude who needed to be taken out.

This was one of the clearest examples of the totalitarian, religious nature of progressivism I had ever witnessed firsthand.

Fortunately, I knew Webb was a good guy—and nothing of what *The Young Turks* crew claimed him to be. As a result, I was disgusted by their behavior, but my feelings of revulsion were also wrapped up in confusion, which initially kept me from speaking up. Looking back, this makes me want to go back in time and slap the 2013 me. Repeatedly. But at least it was the beginning of my awakening and gave me the unpleasant jolt I needed.

The second flash point event came soon after. It happened in late 2014, when neuroscientist and author Sam Harris appeared on

HBO's *Real Time with Bill Maher* to discuss his book, *Waking Up: A Guide to Spirituality Without Religion.*

For those who aren't familiar with the show's format, Harris, whom I'd never heard of at this point, was brought on for a "protected interview." This meant he wasn't expected to converse with the other guests, including Ben Affleck. He was only booked for a one-on-one with Maher.

The interview started off fine, but quickly got hijacked when Harris made the reasonable distinction between criticizing people and ideas, including religious beliefs.

"We've been sold this meme of Islamophobia, where criticism of the religion gets conflated with bigotry towards Muslims as people," he said. "It's intellectually ridiculous."

Before anyone had time to draw breath, an agitated Affleck jumped in. But instead of contributing to the conversation like a grown-up, he basically shouted Harris and Maher down and called them racists, which has now become a standard debating tactic for most progressives.

"Are you the person who officially understands the codified doctrine of Islam?" Affleck peacocked at Harris. The audience fell silent.

"Why are you so hostile?" Maher replied, perturbed. "Because it's gross and racist," Affleck shot back, hackles raised, like a toddler having a tantrum and throwing his toys out of the stroller.

I should point out here that this tactic is typical of people who don't know what they're talking about. Instead of having a solid argument based on fact, they simply moralize their way through life—shouting people down and throwing loaded terms around as a distraction.

Their over-the-top emotion is enough to convince unthinking people on a base level. They've won, because it *appears* as if they're morally right.

Keen to capture this incident in the moment, I leapt from my sofa, grabbed my notebook, and began scribbling down thoughts as the conversation continued to derail. Suddenly, everything I'd been thinking privately about the dysfunction of the progressive mind was bursting forth right in front of my eyes. And not only that, but this manifestation of lefty hysteria was Batman vs. both my favorite comedian and a mild-mannered scientist. I had never seen anything like it.

Still ranting, Affleck became increasingly red-faced and short-tempered as he gave the performance of his life, playing to the gallery. "More than a billion people [Muslims] aren't fanatical!" he added, totally missing Harris's point. "It's stereotyping!"

It was crazy to watch a seemingly respected and evolved adult behave this way. Especially when the media's subsequent reaction was equally nuts.

Specifically, the media turned on Maher overnight. For years, he'd been the standard-bearer of the left. He'd long supported the legalization of pot, universal health care, global-warming initiatives, and voted Democrat. He'd also been fiercely outspoken about Republicans throughout his thirty-year career.

Nonetheless, Maher instantly became public enemy number one after Affleck played the race card. The entire media establishment now hated him, with newspapers such as *The Guardian* painting him as a zealot. It didn't matter how much he'd supported left-wing politics before, or how much he'd scolded conservatives, all that was disqualified and Maher was now "other."

Looking back, I should probably thank Affleck for this. He inadvertently became the blunt instrument that hit sane people over the head. Yes, it was an alarm bell for me, and unfair to Maher and Harris, but this eight-minute clip was also a political awakening for millions of others. Once seen, it couldn't be "unseen."

As the press attention calmed, I hoped the incident would cause progressives to look in the mirror, self-correct, and moderate their behavior.

Sadly, this didn't happen. It fact, it only got worse . . .

Just a few months later, Paris was rocked by the terrorist attacks against satirical magazine *Charlie Hebdo*, which became the third and final event to lead to my awakening.

For centuries, France has enjoyed a rich history of satire. Way before the French Revolution of 1789, which saw Marie Antoinette roasted for her bling lifestyle as poor Parisians starved, buffoons would often poke fun at the establishment, including royalty.

Later, these crazy jesters were replaced by writers. And as technology advanced, other forms of satire began to emerge. By 1970, *Hebdo* was born. The magazine embodied everything a healthy society should; it had no sacred cows and was an equal opportunist when poking fun at power.

This is how it's supposed to be. If we're going to confront reality honestly, then nothing can be off-limits. Our power structures, our political leaders, and our religious institutions all must be fair game in a free society. There's a fine line when jokes and mockery become cruel and pointless, but this is the line comedians have toed since the beginning of time. We must relentlessly defend their ability not only to push our limits but also to occasionally trip over the line into sacrilege and controversy.

Opposition to this belief turned into tragedy on January 7, 2015, when two Al Qaeda operatives, Saïd and Chérif Kouachi, stormed the magazine's editorial offices with Kalashnikov rifles and opened fire, killing twelve innocent people.

Some suggested victims were shot in the face at point-blank range to ensure maximum gore, while others said staff played dead next to their slaughtered colleagues in order to survive. Their blood-stained bodies entangled with corpses.

The motive? Editors had republished cartoons of Muhammad, which the killers considered sacrilegious.

This horrific incident plunged France into national mourning, with then-president François Hollande calling it "an attack on free speech."

World leaders even joined more than one million people on the streets of Paris in peaceful protest. But instead of voicing unequivocal condemnation of the terrorists (like any sane person would), my fellow lefties *defended* them. Yup, you read that correctly—they said criticism of the gunmen would be "Islamophobic" and implied the dead had it coming for being "provocative"!

At that very moment I realized just how high the stakes were. The left had lost it to a dangerous degree.

If a member of the Westboro Baptist Church had opened fire in a U.S. mosque, leftists would be all over it, declaring racism an epidemic, with Christianity to blame. But, in this case, they blamed the cartoonists, excused the murderers, and showed more sympathy for the Muslim community rather than the deceased, whose bodies were still warm.

Of course, virtually all of mainstream media took the bait.

Various outlets, from *BuzzFeed* to *The Huffington Post*, ran with this warped response, and as the world mourned with the French people, I distinctly recall CNN asking whether it was "acceptable" to draw cartoons of religious figures—something it had no problem with when *Hebdo* previously depicted the pope holding a condom and Kim Jong Un flanked by a bare butt.

Suddenly, out of nowhere, rationalizing Islamic terror had become a progressive position. According to progressives, it was another 2-D argument: brown people = good, white people = bad.

These three incidents—the attack on my friend David Webb, Ben Affleck's self-righteous moralizing (the sort only an A-list Hollywood star could do!), and the desire to obfuscate Islamic terror—became the holy trinity of left-wing lunacy that set me on the course to divorcing the deluded from my life.

Initially, I thought I was alone in my political awakening and feared that it might always be this way, but soon enough, others also got mugged by reality.

Professor Bret Weinsten was one of them. A revered academic at Evergreen State College in Washington—arguably the most "woke" school in America—Weinsten was a die-hard progressive who earned his credentials supporting the Occupy Wall Street protests and even begged forgiveness for merely voting in the 2016 election. No kidding.

"It would be pointless to attempt to apologize to everyone who might have been hurt by my vote," he wrote for medium.com. "But I believe it is important to go through the exercise of genuinely recognizing the harm my choice invited, and to signify that I understand the debt it implies."

You might think this would safeguard him from the mob—especially as he voted for Clinton, not Trump—but you'd be wrong.

They still sacrificed him in May 2017, when he opposed racial segregation.

For context, Evergreen College has long held a "Day of Absence" in which people of color boycott the campus to protest racism. As a die-hard progressive, Weinstein always supported this, but he objected when activists flipped the script and wanted all white people—both faculty and students—to leave the college for twenty-four hours as admission of their "supremacy."

He politely refused, saying he understood their motives, but questioned the approach. Choosing not to attend classes is one thing, he said, but forcing others out is another.

As you might've guessed, this reasoned response caused mass hysteria. Think *The Walking Dead,* but with more zombies. Gangs of students (most of whom he'd never taught) began protesting his office, hurling accusations of racism and demanding he be sacked—*for having a different opinion.* They even stopped traffic and searched cars while carrying baseball bats.

Eventually, the witch hunt got so bad that Weinstein and his wife, Heather Heying (also a biology professor at Evergreen), were forced from their jobs and banished into exile almost overnight.

"I tried to reason with [these students]. I felt no fear because I knew that whatever my failings might be, bigotry was not among them," he later told Congress in a special address. "At that moment I felt sure I could reach them. I felt a moral obligation to explain that racism squanders potential and erodes dignity. I'm also well versed in the evolutionary logic that makes racism durable, so should've had no trouble establishing common ground, [but] the protesters had no interest in the very dialogue they seemed to invite."

Their ultimate goal, he says, is to silence dissent—and they're succeeding.

"One's right to speak is now dictated by adherence to an ascendant orthodoxy in which one's race, gender, and sexual orientation are paramount," Weinstein added.

"[This] is about power and control. Speech is impeded as a last resort when people fail to censor themselves in response to a threat. [This tactic is] being used to unhook the values that bind us together as a nation: equal protection under the law and the presumption of innocence. A free marketplace of ideas. The concept that people should be judged by the content of their character rather than the color of their skin. Yes, even that core tenet of the civil rights movement is being dismantled."

Bret and his wife, Heather, reluctantly settled with Evergreen State and fled Washington altogether, which is terrifying. If it can happen to them—two lifelong progressives—it can happen to you too.

A similar fate awaited graduate student and teaching assistant Lindsay Shepherd. Another lifelong lefty, she was branded transphobic while lecturing a class at Wilfrid Laurier University in Ontario, Canada.

The accusation came after she dared to show footage of a little-known Canadian psychology professor named Jordan Peterson discussing gender pronouns (FYI, Peterson has repeatedly stated that he is fully supportive of transgender rights; he just doesn't want government-enforced rules on speech).

Raked over the coals in a disciplinary meeting, Shepherd was accused by senior staff of creating a "toxic climate for students" and enforcing heteronormative standards.

Wisely, she secretly recorded the conversation, which later saved her ass from a number of crazy accusations—namely, that her behavior was contrary to both the university's policy on sexual violence and the Ontario Human Rights Code.

An investigation later revealed that no such breaches ever happened. What *did* happen, however, was that she bravely stood up to the mob—and survived.

Later that same year, leftists went after a new target: software engineer James Damore. This time, however, it wasn't hormonal students or morally corrupt academics who were leading the charge. It was Silicon Valley, the gatekeepers of all the information we consume.

Damore's targeting happened after he provided feedback on Google's diversity program, which claims STEM (science, technology, engineering, and mathematics) is rife with sexism.

In a now famous memo titled "Google's Ideological Echo Chamber: How Bias Clouds Our Thinking about Diversity and Inclusion," Damore counterargued that the genders are biologically different and, as a result, often gravitate toward different careers. Not always, but generally speaking.

Furthermore, he said this was OK. Biology isn't bigotry, people!

I should clarify here that Damore was a model employee before this fiasco. Not only had he been headhunted from Harvard but also he'd been promoted just months before "Memogate."

Furthermore, his observations were rooted in science, not sexism. Researchers at the University of Missouri had found a "gender equality paradox" when they studied 475,000 teenagers across the globe. They noted that hyperegalitarian countries such as Finland, Norway, and Sweden had a smaller percentage of female STEM

DON'T BURN THIS BOOK

graduates than countries such as Albania and Algeria, which are considered less advanced.

In other words, the more "gender equality" a place had, the more men and women chose traditional gender roles. But none of this mattered to one of the world's biggest companies, Google, which fired Damore in August 2017.

"Part of building an open, inclusive environment means fostering a culture in which those with alternative views, including different political views, feel safe sharing their opinions," said Google's VP of Diversity, Danielle Brown. "But that discourse needs to work alongside the principles of equal employment found in our Code of Conduct, policies, and antidiscrimination laws."

In other words, free speech is good—unless you say something "bad." Poor George Orwell must've been spinning in his grave.

Making matters worse, journalists then painted Damore as a sexist pig who revels in controversy, which couldn't have been further from the truth.

He hadn't written that memo for attention or notoriety. He was simply doing his due diligence as an employee by providing the feedback *they'd* requested from a mandatory meeting *they'd* hosted. Hardly incentive for other employees to provide feedback in the future.

When Damore appeared on the *The Rubin Report* a few weeks later, he was the most reserved, unassuming, and timid guest I'd ever had. I personally had to spend thirty minutes in the green-room trying to get him to relax before we began recording, something I've never done before or since with anyone else.

The whole debacle was unnecessary, but I developed mixed feelings about this specific incident.

Naturally, I was appalled by Google's spineless behavior, but it also had an upside. Like a silver lining behind a storm cloud, it confirmed what I suspected all along: that the problem was the progressive left, not me.

Better still, I was in extraordinarily good company with some genuine freethinkers and amazing minds.

This unconditional sense of community is one of the best benefits of being rejected, or expelled, by progressives. But it's certainly not the only one. So, in case you're not aware of them, let me tell you about some of the other surprising upsides . . .

First, there are now *millions* of us out here, which means somebody's always got your back. How do I know this? Because I've met many of the people who are now "us." From the streets of Amsterdam to the supermarkets of Australia and the crowded trains of Copenhagen, I've had frank conversations with good folk who've also been cast out for having original thoughts.

One was a member of the Gay Men's Chorus of Los Angeles, who was cold-shouldered from the group after being outed as a log-cabin conservative. Another was an Emmy Award–winning set designer who—being a straight white man—was told his services were no longer required because a person of color would do a better job. A third was a woman in London who reluctantly removed her child from school because of the abuse he got for his Brexit-voting family.

The one thing they all had in common? Once they survived the initial shame and pain of rejection, they all viewed their banishment as a blessing in disguise. Why? Because it finally opened their eyes to the reality of the situation. It stopped them from playing a tedious game that they could never win—because it's designed to fail.

They also noticed that it's so much cooler out here on the fringe, which is true. Free-thinking is the new counterculture, which makes it cutting-edge and subversive, like punk rock or hip-hop in the early 1980s. It's on the periphery where all the sexy, rebellious, and exciting stuff happens, not the mainstream center left, which has become like an R-rated movie stripped down to PG for minimum offense.

Last but not least, here's the best bit: Independent thinking actually makes you more attractive. No kidding, brains are sexy. See, groupthink is basic and that's not hot! It requires absolutely no thought, no courage, no chutzpah. Conversely, owning your own mind is infinitely more appealing.

Trust me, beauty fades, but dumb is forever.

This is all worth remembering when you inevitably face your own experience with the progressive mob (if you haven't already, of course). You might be a kid who's scared to speak up in class, a lipstick lesbian who dares to champion the Second Amendment, or a Trump supporter who lives in the People's Republic of California. Whatever your story, it's all good.

The left may no longer be liberal, but you're no longer left out.

3

Think Freely or Die

F REE-THINKING IS TRICKY. There isn't a road map that delivers you to the site of a set destination.

It's actually more like being a nomad than a settler: there's no political party for you to call a permanent home.

Although this might sound scary, it's actually incredibly liberating.

See, free-thinking is fluid. Unlike our bloated political system, it's creative and keeps your mind agile. In fact, the tribal political game and free-thinking are at complete odds with each other.

One requires conformity, while the other is impossible to pigeonhole.

The more I learned to consider each individual political issue on its merits, without the influence of progressive groupthink, the better I felt—the more *enlightened* I felt. I didn't want to be part of a group that relies on the whims and emotions of the masses anymore. Although I didn't realize it at the time, I was in fact returning to the roots I grew up with: the roots of true liberalism.

Before this realization, I thought loyalty to the progressive agenda was the job of a good liberal, but it's actually the death of true, old-fashioned, classical liberalism. In only two shorts years, I realized that progressivism was a dead end, and it was time to go my own way.

(Cue Fleetwood Mac's "Go Your Own Way.")

True liberalism, classical liberalism, was the political philosophy I was looking for. I'd been temporarily mind-hijacked by progressivism because it seemed like a louder, sexier liberalism.

I returned with a new appreciation for classically liberal values. Sure, I'd dumped them for a newer model—but they were the original and best. (New Coke is to Classic Coke as progressivism is to classical liberalism.)

Then, as any YouTuber worth their salt does, I just started talking about the ideas I believe in. Next thing I knew, everywhere I went, whether it was the supermarket, the movie theater, or the mall, people were always asking me, "So Dave, what exactly is a classical liberal?"

I wondered how America's founding political philosophy became lost on us—even on people who called themselves "liberals." Three years after my awakening, I still get this question all the time. So what better place to officially answer it than in my very own book?

A classical liberal sounds like someone who's liberal, but fancier. Perhaps the sort of guy who sports a top hat, a mustache, and a monocle, but there's much more to it than that.

The formal definition of the term is "a political philosophy and ideology belonging to liberalism, in which primary emphasis is placed on securing the freedom of the individual by limiting the power of the government."

Said more simply, it's "live and let live."

This notion was born from some of history's greatest thinkers, including John Locke, Adam Smith, John Stuart Mill, and Thomas Jefferson. While they all tinkered in their own way with the ideas of classical liberalism, the core belief—that the protection of individual rights is the most pressing political priority—remained constant.

Jefferson even threw "the pursuit of happiness" into the Declaration of Independence to drive home the point that your happiness wasn't the government's to give, but rather yours to take.

Putting the individual above the group not only empowers you to live your life as you see fit, but it also neutralizes the bigotry of stereotyping—"Black people are lazy! Mexicans are criminals! Jews are cheap!," etc.

Think about yourself right now. Do you represent all white people, or black people, or straight people, or gay people? No, of course not. You only represent yourself.

Segregating Americans into identity groups—the very essence of bigotry—has been fully embraced by modern progressivism, which has absolutely nothing to do with classical liberalism.

Progressivism has traded a love of individual rights for paternalistic, insincere concern for the collective. It judges people based upon their skin color, gender, and sexuality, thus imagining them as competitors in an Oppression Olympics in which victimhood is virtue.

We no longer accept that "all men are created equal." We've abandoned this liberal, enlightened idea for a postmodern one—one that says we have no shared roots, hence the obsession with race, gender, and immutable characteristics. This postmodern view of the world cannot create anything—it can only deconstruct and divide. While liberalism aims to produce hard work and pride around a common cause, our new, negative worldview spawns only jealousy and grievance.

I would rather be defined by what I support than what I oppose.

Hence I'm dedicating the next few pages to spell this out, issue by issue, in straight-talking detail. I don't want us to get lost in the morass of daily politics, but I do want us to be able to assert the classically liberal position on the important issues of the day.

Whether you agree with me on all of these topics is irrelevant, as long as you've put in the work to figure out what you truly believe, rather than just accepting the mainstream narrative.

And remember, a political philosophy (in this case classical liberalism) is very different from a political party platform. A philosophy frames an argument, but a platform lays out specific policies.

Once you know your own political philosophy, it is then your job as a freethinker to decide for yourself which (if any) party best embodies the values you believe in. Consider this an acid test for your ideals.

I suspect you'll end up identifying as a classical liberal by the time you're done with this chapter, but I'll let you decide for yourself.

DRUGS

I've done a pretty decent amount of drugs in my day.

I've smoked pot, snorted coke, eaten magic mushrooms. I've danced (poorly) on ecstasy and probably a couple other things. These days I'm a red wine and indica guy, but I don't deny my past. Actually, I have some great memories of it; though probably can't remember some of it for the very same reasons.

So it's probably no surprise that I believe people should be free to decide their own drug intake without risk of being locked up.

Let's start with the easiest one here, marijuana. It is a fact that there has never, ever been a recorded death from smoking a joint. Actually, cannabis can have some surprising health benefits.

Medical science has done incredible research into how CBD (cannabidiol—an extract from the plant) can help people in a whole host of ways, from shrinking cancerous tumors to managing autism, alleviating the symptoms of Alzheimer's disease, and curbing anxiety. CBD is the nonpsychotropic compound found in the marijuana plant, so you can get these health benefits with no fear of getting high.

When my fourteen-year-old dog, Emma, got bladder cancer back in February 2019, my husband, David, and I had a choice to make: to put her through chemo, radiation, and a series of intense drugs with a small chance of shrinking the tumor, or to go another route altogether. After factoring in her advanced age, we decided not to put her on any conventional medicine but rather chose a natural route that included CBD and mushroom supplements. The vet's prognosis was that Emma probably had two weeks to five months to live, even with conventional treatment. As of this writing, she is nine months strong since the diagnosis and is doing just great. I know this is anecdotal, but I'm just happy to write it.

Of course, even if none of the human or canine health benefits of marijuana existed, I'd still champion its legalization because you can smoke, eat, or drink what you want. (Yes, marijuana now comes in all these forms, plus gels, creams, and waxes.)

Besides, we already have two declassified drugs that are far more dangerous: alcohol and nicotine.

There were eighty-eight thousand alcohol-related deaths each year in the United States from 2006 to 2010, shortening the lives of those who died by an average of three decades. Then there's all of the DUIs, domestic violence incidents, and nonlethal injuries that it's responsible for. Plus the economic costs, which—according to the Centers for Disease Control and Prevention—were a whopping $249 billion in 2010 alone.

Nicotine isn't so innocent either. Although arguably less dangerous, its use can be associated with cardiovascular disease, birth defects, poisoning, and inflammation. Some experts even fear it can lead to type 2 diabetes and increased blood pressure.

So if you're pro-beer and happy to smoke cigarettes, yet opposed to people having the occasional blunt, then you have some seriously muddled principles, my friend.

My perspective is this: adults should be free to consume whatever they want, whenever they want, as long as there are no consequences for other people.

The catch is that this libertarian-inspired view falls apart when it starts to include Schedule I substances such as crack and heroin, which are obviously very different beasts. These substances are highly addictive and frequently fatal, and can inspire a whole host of criminal activity along the way, which is where the lightest possible touch of government comes into play.

In these instances, I'm reluctantly OK for the state to make a judgment call, because freedom can't be a free-for-all. Sure, we want to give people maximum liberties, but we also don't want a *Breaking Bad* episode happening next door, with half the local population whacked-out on meth. That's not the key to a healthy, functioning society.

Take a walk through San Francisco if you want to see the

horrors of what highly addictive drugs like meth and opiates do to people and the community at large. It ain't pretty, and unfortunately it's on the government to make sure it doesn't spiral completely out of control.

I know the hardcore libertarians will find this compromise a hard pill to swallow (pun intended), but we can only go to where the evidence takes us. As we've repeatedly seen, human beings have a track record of succumbing to indulgence—and then going off the rails into oblivion. Just look at the likes of Whitney Houston, Amy Winehouse, Michael Jackson, Philip Seymour Hoffman, Heath Ledger, and Prince (actually, maybe the lesson here is to stay far away from the entertainment industry).

While we can't stop people from obtaining illegal drugs—and in almost every case antidrug laws create a black market for them anyway—we must have some line in the sand drawn, both within our minds as individuals and within a legal framework as a society.

As we lay out these laws, however, we should give the devil his due. So let's look a bit deeper at how laws and taxation on vices have affected us.

The New York State tax on a pack of twenty cigarettes is $4.35, while NY City tax is $1.50, comprising $5.85 of the $14 total. The result? Yup, you guessed it, New York is now the black market capital in the United States for illegal cigarette sales.

It's not just the black market that these well-intentioned drug laws create though. There's also a personal element to it here, which is that we are penalizing people for what often becomes their only momentary escape—their right to relax in life. Is that really what the government is in business for?

"But, Dave, it seems like you're saying two competing things here. You want some drugs to be legal yet you acknowledge that when you make other drugs illegal there are unintended personal and criminal consequences. How does that make sense?"

Good question. I'm glad you asked!

The ideal here would be that nobody would abuse drugs—ever—and that everyone who chooses to use them would consume them in moderation. But we all know this isn't a realistic public policy. While libertarians err on the side of absolute personal choice here, I believe that some minimal governmental guidelines are appropriate to better ensure we don't become a nation of addicts. This is where my belief in individual liberty conflicts with the notion of creating a stable, functioning society. Thus the light touch of government.

Interestingly, I'd be happy to be proven wrong here. Maybe there is some utopian alternative; perhaps there's a Burning Man–type city in which every drug known to humankind would be legal and work out just fine. But I suspect not.

Until this happens, the best compromise is to remove all federal restrictions and kick everything back to individual states.

If some states want to completely declassify everything, then so be it—it's their choice, just as it's your choice to leave if you are unhappy with their decision. And conversely, if some states want stricter drug laws, then they should be allowed to as well. The key here is that it isn't a federal one-size-fits-all policy but rather something that is brought to the local level, where you, the citizen, will have more of a voice in shaping the laws of the place you live in.

This way, the American experiment is constantly ongoing, with all the options being road-tested for our broader consideration.

Whether you want to be stoned during that experiment is up to you.

GAY MARRIAGE

Take it from a dude, who happens to be married to a dude, who knows from personal experience, the whole gay marriage thing is a no-brainer from a classical liberal perspective.

It goes a little something like this: if you believe in individual rights—meaning that every citizen of a country should expect the same legal privileges and protections, whether or not you agree with their choices—then, great stuff, you're on the right path.

But before you join that conga line in celebration, there's a catch: all of this means absolutely nothing unless you're willing to tolerate somebody else's personal opposition to it.

No, I'm not kidding and, no, this isn't a device to test your concentration levels. It's something called a consistent principle and is frequently the undoing of well-meaning (but ultimately misguided) progressives, who falter and then fall into authoritarianism.

Let me explain why . . .

Part of being a true, classical liberal is accepting that many people have fundamental objections to homosexuality because of their religious faith. You might not like their views—hey, you might even think they're pretty old-fashioned—but that's irrelevant. Like you, these people are entitled to their own outlook.

It only becomes a problem if they try to stop you from exercising your equal rights under the law.

This is something that relates back to the First Amendment, which clearly sets out the importance of freedom of religion and assembly for everyone . . . including those you disagree with. This is what it means to be equal. No special treatment for anyone.

Think of it this way: I wouldn't force a Jewish painter to take commissions of Hitler imagery from a Nazi sympathizer. And I'd bet you wouldn't either. Nor would I make it mandatory for a historically black church to hold an event for white supremacists. This isn't rocket science, people.

I also wouldn't take legal action against a Christian baker if the baker politely refused to create my rainbow-themed wedding cake. (For the record, we had a simple lemon and rosemary cake at the wedding, baked by my mother-in-law. Sorry to break the stereotype.)

Unfortunately, as we witnessed in the legal case against Melissa and Aaron Klein—the now-infamous wedding cake bakers, or non-bakers, as it were—progressives have decided that if you don't run your business the way they want you to, they will take legal action against you. Without relitigating that whole affair, it's important to note that the Kleins didn't refuse service to the gay couple, they just refused a custom order of a cake.

This is a crucial distinction, because refusing service based on immutable characteristics might've been a violation of the Civil Rights Act of 1964, which ended segregation and banned employment discrimination on the basis of race, color, religion, sex, and national origin. Although sexuality is not specifically mentioned here, there could've been a legal case to be had. (And it should be noted that there are several other laws currently in place, such as the Equality Act of 1974, that protect people based specifically on sexuality.)

This overreaction is precisely the sort of irrational behavior we've been witnessing from the overzealous left in recent years. Its adherents want any form of dissent to be classified as a criminal act and punishable by law, even if that means making somebody unemployed, which is illiberal, and thankfully illegal, for now.

In a liberal society people have the right to hold different beliefs than yours. That right is what we must protect above all else.

Look at my friendship with Ben Shapiro, for example. He's an Orthodox Jew who doesn't personally agree with gay marriage because of his devout faith. In fact, he flat-out describes my lifestyle as a sin. Surprise, surprise, I disagree with him on this view, but this isn't a problem for me because (A) we accept that our different opinions are of equal worth, and (B) he's not trying to overturn the law or infringe on my rights.

Likewise, I'm not forcing his synagogue to host a lesbian commitment ceremony against its religious principles. Nor am I forcing him to shack up with a dude and listen to Tina Turner playlists on loop. Yes, I'm more of a Tina guy than a Beyoncé guy. Sue me, gays.

I view my disagreement with Ben this way because my rights as an individual don't trump somebody else's, just like that person's freedoms don't supersede mine. See how it works? It's mutually beneficial for everyone involved.

It's our responsibility as free-thinking, self-determining people to pursue our own happiness without forcing others to bow to our beliefs. Especially when it might come at their expense.

This concept is so easy to understand that it's a piece of (gay) cake.

IMMIGRATION

I wouldn't dream of getting off a flight into another country, swaggering up to the passport control, and demanding permanent residency.

This would make me an entitled buffoon who fulfills all the clichés of the brash, vulgar American.

It'd also be hugely unfair to dump myself on the hardworking citizens of a foreign land, who've spent decades building their infrastructure and refining their culture through blood, sweat, tears, and taxation—to which I've contributed absolutely nothing.

Therefore, it doesn't take a genius to understand that they'd be entirely justified in turning me away without being branded racist, far-right xenophobes who suffer from "fragility" of whatever sort.

This, dear reader, is precisely why I believe in nation-states. Just like an individual should be able to determine their own fate, so too should the country in which they live. Even if this means deporting my sorry ass on the very next passenger plane.

This is nationalism, loyalty and devotion to one's country, in the true sense and embodies many fundamental tenets of classical liberalism.

"It's a principled standpoint that sees the world governed best when it consists of many independent nations, which have their own laws, traditions, language, and religious customs which aren't forced to live a certain way by other nations," said Yoram Hazony, author of *The Virtue of Nationalism*, during his *Rubin Report* appearance in 2018. And he's absolutely correct.

This commonsense approach transcends race to apply everywhere, from Japan to Poland, Australia, and—dare I say it—even the United States of America. If you struggle with this concept, it might be because you think borders are bad. But they aren't.

Borders are all around us in various forms—they're the laws that stop criminals from stealing our property, the front doors that keep us safe at night, and the parameters of personal space that discourage people from getting in our faces.

Even literal borders are good. The triple-fence erected along San Diego's U.S.-Mexican border has been hugely successful, reducing illegal access by 90 percent. Likewise, Israel's border wall with the West Bank is considered another triumph for its citizens. Before its existence, Israel suffered countless suicide bombings, which terrorized thousands of innocent people.

Now, this problem has almost completely been eradicated.

Since then, other nations throughout Europe have built their own territory markers, including Spain, Greece, Norway, Hungary, Macedonia, and Austria. Are these countries racist? Are they building walls in the name of racism? Of course not. They've simply seen the resulting chaos of the alternative and responded proportionately.

When Germany's chancellor Angela Merkel welcomed millions of immigrants from Iraq, Syria, Afghanistan, and other troubled nations, it cost the nation billions *per year* for government-funded shelters, dental care, and cost-of-living allowances (which frequently exceeded the minimum wages in neighboring countries).

This largesse might've negated her personal sense of Holocaust guilt, but it also sparked huge assimilation issues, security threats, and crime rates, which is hardly surprising when you consider that many of the "huddled masses" were economic migrants (usually men of fighting age, frequently holding hateful views about Jews, gays, and other infidels) who'd likely been infiltrated by terrorist sympathizers.

Sensible people across the political spectrum knew this policy was a disaster as they watched it unfold, but anybody who tried to sound the alarm was branded a far-right, racist xenophobe.

In the end, it became such an unmitigated disaster that Merkel U-turned on her promise and offered migrants a financial incentive to go back to their original homelands. Take a moment to think about this stunning reversal of policy. One moment Merkel wanted to welcome in millions and give them benefits for the privilege of being Germans, and the next minute she's literally paying them to get the hell out.

That strikes me as more offensive than refusing them entry in the first place. It's like inviting friends over for a party, realizing that they eat too much, and then handing them a cash incentive to leave early.

These events in Merkel's Germany are a perfect example of why applying a moderate level of control benefits everyone. We all know this to be true, but we're often too scared to admit it. Especially when it comes to America.

This doesn't mean I'm advocating for a physical wall across the entire southern border, but—then again—I'm not completely opposed to the idea either (you could say I'm sitting on the fence— waka! waka!). What I *am* saying is that each country has a primary duty to care for its existing population, including the millions of legal immigrants who've already moved there to build a new life and are now part of the community.

This is not a hard-line, far-right message. It's a measured, common-sense compromise that's been espoused historically by a number of Democrats, including Barack Obama and Hillary Clinton.

"We are a generous and welcoming people here in the United States," Obama said in 2005. "But those who enter the country illegally, and those who employ them, disrespect the rule of law, and they are showing disregard for those who are following the law."

He added: "We simply cannot allow people to pour into the United States undetected, undocumented, unchecked, and circumventing the line of people who are waiting patiently, diligently, and lawfully to become immigrants into this country."

A few years later, in a 2013 State of the Union address, Obama promised to put illegal immigrants "to the back of the line."

Real reform means strong border security, and we can build on the progress my administration has already made—putting more boots on the southern border than at any time in our history and reducing illegal crossings to their lowest levels in forty years.

Real reform means establishing a responsible pathway to earned citizenship—a path that includes passing a background check, paying taxes and a meaningful penalty, learning English, and going to the back of the line behind the folks trying to come here legally.

He even once told ABC's George Stephanopoulos: "Our direct message to families is 'do not send your children to the border.' If they do make it, they'll be sent back. But they may not make it [at all]."

Yes, that's progressive hero, Mr. Hope and Change himself, Barack Obama, sounding an awful lot like evil, racist Republican Donald Trump, wouldn't you say?

Meanwhile, Democrat senator Chuck Schumer of New York once said during a 2009 speech at Georgetown University: "The American people are fundamentally pro-legal immigration and anti-illegal immigration. We will only pass comprehensive reform when we recognize this fundamental concept.

"First, illegal immigration is wrong. A primary goal of comprehensive immigration reform must be to dramatically curtail future illegal immigration."

Then, nervous Nancy Pelosi added: "We all agree we need to secure our borders, while honoring our values."

Even Democrat senator Dianne Feinstein of California criticized the flood of migrants coming from Mexico. Speaking during a visit to the border in the early 1990s, she said: "It's a competition for space. Whether the space is a job, the space is a home, a place in a classroom, it becomes a competition for space."

Boy, these people are seriously racist (according to their own self-proclaimed standards of today). Despite this hypocrisy, I will actually defend them as they throw their former selves under the bus.

Everything they all said above was true. And we all know it. Now it's just become politically expedient to say the opposite because of the "bad orange man" in the White House.

But they were all right years ago: part of the reason for controlling the borders is to make sure that we can actually deliver our "American dream" promise.

Many blue-collar jobs are currently being replaced by automation, which means lots of low-skilled labor workers (many of them refugees) are at risk of being unemployed and on handouts. Is this ethical? To invite people into our country just to have them flounder? I don't think so.

We'd also have mainstream Democrat politicians gaslighting them by saying they're victims for coming here in the first place. After all, America is (apparently) an evil, racist patriarchy that hates immigrants, legal or otherwise.

Amazingly though, everyone still wants to come and live here.

Those other countries must be really horrible to be worse than ours is!

As if that wasn't enough, the regressive left also loves to conflate nationalism with racism, or white nationalism, but its adherents forget one thing—a strong border is a sign of sovereignty. Another term for sovereignty? Self-care. Which is precisely what classical liberalism is all about. By caring for ourselves, we can care for others.

So what is a sensible immigration policy? It's pretty close to what Obama, Schumer, Pelosi, and Feinstein said years ago, which is ironically pretty damn close to what President Trump says today.

Let's secure the border, figure out who is here illegally, and offer them a pathway to citizenship. Likewise, let's take in new immigrants in numbers that will help our economy, rather than make them reliant on the citizens who are already here.

If this makes me a racist xenophobe I suspect I'm in good company.

ABORTION

I'm currently in the process of becoming a father via surrogacy.

One option is that my sister will provide the egg, and my husband, David, will provide the sperm.

Their contributions will be mixed in a lab (which is way more expensive than a bottle of tequila and a Viagra pill) and nine months later a child will be born.

One other option is that we will create embryos from my sperm and my husband's with an anonymous egg donor and have two children, one from each of us.

Before this process started, I'd always been solidly pro-choice, though in the last two years or so I've begun to describe myself as "begrudgingly pro-choice" after learning more about the biology of gestation and the process of abortion and seeing the left fetishize it in a way that I'm not comfortable with.

There are countless videos on YouTube of women celebrating their terminations, while organizations such as Shout Your Abortion encourages Twitter users to do the same with carefree abandon . . . of course using colorful, eye-catching images.

One woman, who implied she was having an affair with a married man, posted: "When I have a baby in the future, it will be with a man who loves us, respects us, and is honest with us. I will have a baby to start a family, not unintentionally break one up."

Yes, this person is actually saying that she would rather end a life than end a marriage.

Another woman proudly declared: "I wasn't ready to start over again. People can call it selfish or sinful, but at the end of the day, they're not the one tending to my kids."

Then, without a shred of irony, she added: "I want to execute my goals once because I never got the chance to when I stayed at home with my child."

Execute, indeed.

For me, this is incredibly odd and divorced from reality. See, David and I have met with enough doctors and professionals to know that life begins the moment sperm fertilizes the egg. Like it or not, this is the genesis of life.

If it wasn't "alive," why would we be putting a fertilized egg into the surrogate in the first place? Trust me, I can find other ways to spend $150,000.

Yet, despite this incontrovertible truth, I still support the right of women to have an abortion. Abortions should be "safe and rare," said Leana Wen, the recently canceled president of Planned Parenthood.

What may seem to be a logical inconsistency is a well-thought-out position that I've had to discuss with my husband and family many times.

What if early in the pregnancy we found out that the baby was going to be severely physically or mentally disabled, unable to ever live an independent, fully realized life?

We've spent hours discussing how this would not only affect the human being we're bringing into the world but also ourselves and extended families. If early on we could detect such abnormalities, we decided that we would terminate the pregnancy.

You can judge me for this—and I can judge myself—but it's a personal decision we made after balancing not only the potential for the baby's life but also the impact it would have on us as a family.

Would it be an easy decision for us to make? No, not at all. It would be almost impossibly difficult. Would I wrestle with the consequences for years afterward? Absolutely, yes.

But do I still believe it's an ethically viable act when performed within a reasonable time frame? Yes, I do.

Like I always say, two things can be true at the same time. And this is one of those cases.

Personally, I've come to believe that a twelve-week time limit is the optimal compromise between observing the rights of the individual (primarily the mother, then the baby) and the necessary role of public policy, which protects our freedoms in the first place.

This is a situation in which personal views of morality and public standards of law butt heads in an intractable opposition. My libertarian side says that government should have nothing to do with this decision, but my realist side says the state has a duty to protect the life of the unborn. The question here is when.

We know that fetuses begin to transform from a cluster of cells into a recognizable human at three months. After this point they display fully developed eyes, hands, arms, feet, fingers, and toes, plus nails and earlobes.

Most of their internal organs are also detectable, including a beating heart—surely if you ignore all of those other characteristics, you cannot ignore this one.

Not only is twelve weeks more than enough time for a woman to make this personal decision, but as noted above, the fetus really begins what we could call human development at this time. My previous position of five months was based on when it's known a fetus can feel pain, but I no longer believe that to be a tenable position.

According to studies between 2003 and 2005, 20 to 35 percent of babies born at 24 weeks survive, while 50 to 70 percent of babies born at 25 weeks, and more than 90 percent born at 26 to 27 weeks, survive. My 20-week cutoff point was just too close to these horrifying statistics.

If 20 to 35 percent of babies born at twenty-four weeks can survive, I cannot in good conscience be for a public policy that would have them aborted just four weeks earlier.

With this in mind, I believe the classically liberal approach to abortion comes down to if and when one personally decides it's OK to have an abortion.

This is the constant push and pull between the private and the public. My position of twelve weeks puts the focus on the mother up until a point, then says the government must protect the life of the child beginning at that point.

When the issue is viewed through this lens, I think we can have a powerful debate as to whether the twelve-week marker is fair, or whether it should be six weeks or twenty weeks. I should add that I would also allow certain exceptions after twelve weeks in cases when the fetus's or mother's life are in jeopardy—or if severe abnormalities in the development of the child will unquestionably affect its long-term life. But in no case are late-term abortions without these exceptions acceptable. To terminate a pregnancy at seven or eight months is not only an obvious act of violence, but also a clear violation of a fully-formed individual's right to life.

Classical liberalism doesn't demand that you bow to it. It instructs you to make a decision for yourself. Then, through that process, we can figure out what is best for a society at large.

This is in contrast to the traditional conservative position, which has been firmly pro-life. It is also at odds with the ever-changing position of progressives, which now sees no end to when a woman can have an abortion.

My belief is that the only way to negotiate this complex issue is to make a compromise, even if it will most likely upset people on both sides.

In other words, the belief in individual freedom must extend to having confidence in people making the best decisions for themselves—even if we personally believe they are ethically and morally wrong.

This is the balance between individual rights and the light touch of government. You may not be thrilled with the outcome, but it takes into account the widest set of opinions and tries to offer as much choice as possible, within reason.

Now that everyone is angry at me, let's move on!

FREE SPEECH

Back in 1972, the American Civil Liberties Union defended the right for neo-Nazis to march through the village of Skokie, Illinois—despite the fact it had one of the largest communities of Holocaust survivors in America.

I support this decision completely, despite my painful family history, which I'll get to later.

My stance on this isn't because I enjoy listening to anti-Semitic propaganda or conspiracy theories spewed by true racists, but because I'm a free-speech absolutist. Yes, even when it comes to opinions I find abhorrent. *In fact, specifically when it comes to those opinions.*

The only exceptions to this rule have already been specified by the Supreme Court of the United States: calling for direct violence against a person or specific group, yelling "fire" in a crowded theater (with the intent to incite iminent lawless action), and defaming somebody through libel or slander. Everything else should get a free pass, every single time. No exceptions, ever.

This isn't some willy-nilly principle I use to earn social justice points. It's a rule of thumb I live by every single day.

My beliefs were put to the test during a talk I gave at the University of Arizona in 2017 with friend and former *Rubin Report* guest Michael Shermer, editor of *Skeptic* magazine.

At the top of the debate I polled the audience to see how many conservatives, liberals, libertarians, and progressives were in the crowd. Then, as a joke, I asked how many Nazis were in the room (something I've done before that usually gets a big laugh).

Shockingly, a woman raised her hand and proclaimed that she was, in fact, a Nazi. As awkward laughter spread throughout the room, I told her that if she respectfully listened to us, then I'd give her the microphone first during the Q and A. She obliged and that's just what we did.

She later told us that the Nazis didn't really drop deadly Zyklon-B into the gas chambers of Auschwitz and Treblinka, where millions of victims perished. Her "proof" was that there was no evidence of the drop holes in the ceilings. This was an offshoot of an argument made by notorious Holocaust denier David Irving.

Shermer, who is an expert in debunking conspiracy theories, was more than happy to counter her delusions. He calmly explained to her how the Nazis destroyed much of the physical evidence before the camps were liberated. He also used precise dates and specifics, even mentioning his own visit to Auschwitz.

This exchange was exactly what free expression is all about. The woman was allowed to attend an event and listen to the presenters speak. Then we gave her an opportunity to share her thoughts as well.

Ultimately her ideas were debunked and exposed, and whether she was convinced or not, nobody was silenced, intimidated, or threatened. I sincerely doubt any other audience member was convinced by her, and if anything, hearing Shermer calmly counter her story was a further vindication of the truth.

By respecting the principles of free expression, we deftly proved that free speech is the ultimate disinfectant for bad ideas, which it is. Just as scientists must have their papers peer-reviewed before publication, we too should have our beliefs scrutinized by different opinions.

In doing so, it tests the robustness of our logic and weeds out the nonsense.

One final note on this. It turned out that the Holocaust-denying woman was transgender. Yes, that's right—a trans Holocaust denier. Do with that what you will.

This free exchange of information is essential to a civilized society, but it's rapidly being forgotten in a world of trigger warnings and safe spaces. In many parts of the world, the aforementioned conversation would be deemed illegal because of encroaching "hate speech" laws, which have literally made certain topics off-limits.

Back in 2018, the United Kingdom's Alison Chabloz was convicted on two counts of "causing an offensive, indecent or menacing message" after she posted anti-Semitic songs online.

One described Auschwitz as "a theme park," while another called the gas chambers a "proven hoax."

A few months earlier, Scotland's Mark Meechan—aka Count Dankula—was fined more than $1,000 for contravening the Communications Act 2003 with a video of his girlfriend's pug performing a *Sieg heil!* salute.

Other cases later followed in Australia, Canada, France, Switzerland, and Germany.

Again, you may deem these songs, jokes, or conspiracy theories hateful and evil, and you may well be right, but that doesn't mean people shouldn't be able to express them.

Fortunately, and by design, we here in America aren't subjected to these laws. We're protected by the First Amendment, which is perhaps the greatest man-made law of all time. But heed this warning: it might not always stay this way.

Progressives are slowly taking it upon themselves to police our language on the state's behalf. Their authoritarian approach has already created a chilling effect on good people, who now self-censor in order to avoid being fired from their jobs, dumped by their partners, or ejected from college.

I'd argue in most cases, people aren't silencing themselves over anything as repugnant as Holocaust denial or true racism, but rather basic political beliefs, be it a pro-life position or support for a particular politician.

They're even scared of being "unpersoned" by social media giants such as Facebook, Twitter, and YouTube, who've implemented their own guidelines on what's acceptable for people to say.

As private companies, they're free to do whatever they want, but censorship is not a solution to bad ideas. Silencing people never reforms them—it simply pushes their bad ideas underground, where they're allowed to fester and grow, like a tumor. It also makes those censored believe that they are victims, which can fuel paranoid delusions.

The best approach is to allow people to thrash it out in public.

The controversy over NFL star Colin Kaepernick kneeling for the national anthem is a good example of how letting everyone say their piece is the best way to deal with controversial issues.

While most in the media said his spat with Trump was an assault on free speech, I argued that it was the exact opposite. Kaepernick was allowed to kneel for the national anthem just as the president was allowed to criticize him for doing so. (People often forget that the president has the same free speech rights as the rest of us, even if he often exercises those rights in a let's say, umm, provocative way.)

While Trump can say whatever he wants, what he can't do is use the power of the government to force anyone to kneel or do anything else against their conscience.

Meanwhile, the NFL team's owners were then free to decide if they wanted to keep Kaepernick or let him go for being too much of a distraction. The fans also had their say, by either spending their dollars on tickets or spending their money elsewhere.

Nobody was silenced; everybody got to make their point. And whatever the resulting consequences, they were solely based on whatever decision each person had made. This is exactly how it should be.

Free speech and, most important, the prohibition of the government and business being able to control our speech as laid out in the First Amendment are what grant us all of our other rights. That's why it's first, and that's why so many people all over the world are jealous of what we in the United States take for granted.

Let's be sure to speak up when it is being threatened.

GUN CONTROL

Believe it or not, the Founding Fathers were being classically liberal when they penned the U.S. Constitution back in 1787.

Even though they were "evil" white men who shaped the country in their own vision (boo! hiss! etc.), they clearly didn't want the state to rule over its people with unchallenged force.

Instead, they wanted us to have a share of the power if push came to shove. Hence why they explicitly stated in the Second Amendment the following: "A well-regulated militia, being necessary to the security of a free state, the right of the people to keep and bear arms, shall not be infringed."

Take a moment to appreciate this: these guys had the foresight to guarantee you—yes, person reading this, you—the freedom to protect yourself from other citizens and the state, if necessary.

Why did they bother? Because they understood that while power

THINK FREELY OR DIE

corrupts, absolute power corrupts absolutely. Thus, by allowing the American people to be individually armed, it provided everyone with a mutually moderating force.

In other words, our "life, liberty and the pursuit of happiness" is not just something for us to reach for, but it's also something we should have the means to protect for ourselves.

Realistically, it's pretty unlikely that we're going to form a militia and revolt anytime soon, but let's face it: a group of passionate people with weapons can withstand some degree of tyranny if it presents itself. And, for all we know, it might.

Part of being a classical liberal is having a healthy skepticism of power, which is essentially what a gun represents. It's a metaphor for the healthy distrust of others.

So, yeah, I'm very much a supporter of the Second Amendment because it endows the individual with an ability to at least keep the government on watch as it tries to encroach on our freedoms.

Taking your defense, at least partially, into your own hands actually increases your freedoms rather than reduces them. This is because self-reliance is one of the things authoritarians try to take away first.

With all that in mind, there's still no denying that America has a major gun violence problem.

Whether we're talking about school shootings, which happen all too often, or the assassination of police officers—such as the 2016 attack in Dallas, which saw five officers murdered—or even terrorist attacks, guns are usually the weapon of choice when the goal is to kill as many people as possible in an indiscriminate manner.

This is why it should be tough to possess any sort of firearm, *which it is.* Yes, believe it or not, it's not easy to obtain a gun in America.

First, you need to be an adult. Federal law states that you must be at least eighteen years old to buy shotguns, rifles, and ammunition, while everything else, such as handguns, can only be sold to people age twenty-one or older.

It also prohibits the sale of weapons to those deemed high risk, such as fugitives, or people suffering from documented mental illness.

These rules also extend to illegal migrants, tourists, people guilty of possessing controlled substances, anyone issued with a restraining order, and military personnel who've been dishonorably discharged. This is a pretty comprehensive list of restrictions, though if you listen to mainstream media, few, if any, of these restrictions exist at all.

In their continued bid for utopia, progressives still demand we enforce more laws—even though they don't necessarily work. You're not gonna believe this, but generally speaking, good guys follow rules while bad guys don't. This creates a bit of a problem for those who think laws and legislation are the answer to everything.

Let's focus on Chicago as a prime example. It has some of the strictest gun legislation in the country, earning a B+ from the Law Center to Prevent Gun Violence (a body that rates each state on its firearm screening process). Yet it still has some of the nation's highest incident rates of gun crime.

In 2016 there were more than 4,000 victims, while gun-related homicides increased by 61 percent between 2015 and 2016. This put the city's homicide rate at 25.1 per 100,000, compared with 14.7 per 100,000 in Philadelphia and 2.3 in New York City.

Could this be a rare glitch in the matrix? Nope. It's actual proof that legislation has limited effect. This is why it's ultimately foolish to think more laws are the answer.

If they were, we'd have already solved the problem.

You're more than welcome to try a nationwide buyback scheme, in which people surrender their weapons in exchange for a reward fee, but see where it gets you. I'd be willing to bet my life savings that it won't be the gang leaders who lay down their arms.

Hey, if you're really feeling optimistic you can even post signs in schools and restaurants that declare them "gun-free zones," but who do you think will abide by these shiny signs? I'm guessing all the moms and dads (and nannies) will, but what about the crazed gunman who wants to get on the cover of *Rolling Stone*? Pretty sure a note on a sign isn't going to deter this person from his or her evil ambitions.

Surely a better use of time (and state money) would be to strengthen existing legislation while examining the psychological underpinnings behind gun violence in the first place, such as drug use, ideology (religious or political), and mental health.

The National Survey on Drug Use and Health, which was administered by the U.S. Department of Health and Human Services, recently surveyed 600,000 young Americans on their well-being. It found that major depression has almost doubled for 21-year-olds from 2009 to 2017, while the number of 22-year-olds who attempted suicide has doubled from 2008 to 2017.

This sort of information is important because the root of our gun problem isn't the weapon itself but the human beings behind them. After all, it's a person who pulls the trigger.

If you think this isn't relevant, it may be worth noting that one of the Columbine, Colorado, shooters, Eric Harris, had Luvox (a Prozac-like, psychotropic medicine) in his bloodstream.

Likewise, Stephen Paddock, the man who slaughtered fifty-eight people in the Las Vegas shooting—the worst in modern American history—had antianxiety medication in his system and had previously been prescribed diazepam.

Meanwhile, Parkland, Florida, shooter, Nikolas Cruz, had been on psychotropic drugs before he embarked on his killing spree as well.

These are facts. Yet we still allow mind-altering medication to be advertised on television, even though their side effects produce all sorts of problems, such as suicidal tendencies, anxiety, and insomnia.

I'm no expert on prescription medicine or mental health, but perhaps focusing on these elements could be a sane place for the debate to go. After all, it maintains our Second Amendment freedoms without ignoring some pivotal factors.

So, OK, let's talk about existing laws and see if they can be tweaked. But let's not pretend that gun violence is something that can be solved solely by laws, or that it can ever be completely eradicated.

The only way we can eradicate human behavior is to eradicate humans, and that strikes me as pretty extreme.

I've sat across from various people on both sides of the gun control argument and realized that there's no easy answer to this exponentially difficult issue.

The best we can do is arm ourselves with a realistic outlook, not take away our constitutional rights in the hopes of some unattainable dream.

TRANS ISSUES

When I was a boy I wanted to be a Decepticon named Soundwave.

Alas, medical science in the 1980s wasn't advanced enough to swap my body for that of a futuristic robot that turned itself into a cassette player.

This devastated the six-year-old me for at least forty-eight hours, maybe even a bit longer. But by the time I became an adult, I was seriously happy that I wasn't given the option at all.

First, I was way too young to make such a big decision. Second, which public bathroom does a Transformer even use these days?

All right, maybe I'm being a little snarky, but the only way I can think of getting into the whole transgender debate is with a little humor. The only other option might be to encourage compassion for trans people and their struggle for dignity, but I would hope this already goes without saying.

So let me present the classically liberal perspective on this issue . . .

Every human being should be free to modify their body however they see fit, *but only when they're an adult.*

Relax! This isn't reverse ageism or far-right transphobia. It's consistent with how we treat all minors who are considered intellectually incapable of reasoned logic. It's why we don't allow kids to get tattoos, buy a firearm, and drink alcohol or smoke until they're a grown-up (and, if you do, then you should expect a visit from Child Protective Services).

The idea behind this isn't random. It's because a young person's frontal lobe—the brain's control panel, which manages problem-solving, judgment, and emotion—takes years to fully develop. The general consensus is that the brain's development is largely finished by eighteen years old and fully complete seven years later.

Until the former, they must defer to us, the adults who know better.

This is a universally held truth, yet we're now allowing record numbers of young children (some as young as four years old) to change their gender through invasive surgery and potent puberty blockers.

Left-wing "journalists" at *Vice* and *BuzzFeed* love to promote this trend because it looks compassionate and progressive, but the medical data suggests that it's far more complex than that.

Don't just take my word for it. Many trans people argue this point too, including former *Rubin Report* guest Blaire White. She transitioned from male to female in her early twenties and hasn't looked back, but she still maintains that it's a decision for adults to make about themselves. Not children.

There are several reasons for this, but it all boils down to mental and physical immaturity.

As she explained during our interview, there are key anatomical aspects to transitioning as an adult. Notably, the depth of a trans woman's vagina is wholly dependent on the size of her penis, pre-surgery. So if she hasn't gone through the teenage growth spurt that comes with puberty, then there often won't be enough tissue for surgeons to work with to create the vagina.

(For the record, I'd have a huge vagina.)

A trans person is also likely be sterile due to excessive hormones after their transitioning process is complete, which is an impossible concept for somebody to appreciate when they're still a child. The obvious question is, What happens if they change their mind and want to detransition at a later date?

According to the U.S. Transgender Survey from 2015—the largest research of its kind in the country—8 percent of the twenty-eight thousand respondents went back to their original birth gender, which suggests the grass isn't always greener.

According to columnist and political commentator Deborah Soh, this isn't surprising. In her previous guise as a scientific sex researcher, she conducted various studies that proved many children naturally outgrow their gender dysphoria by adulthood.

In other words, it's frequently just a phase.

"Gender dysphoria is real and we should have empathy for what they're suffering, but we should also be thinking of the best outcome for the child," she told me during her appearance on *The Rubin Report* in 2018.

"All eleven studies on the topic of desistance [not going through with surgical transition] say the same thing, which is that the vast majority of children, sixty to ninety percent, completely outgrow the desire [to change gender]. They're more likely to grow up to be gay, rather than trans."

For classical liberals, this is where a moderate degree of government legislation would act in the individual's best interests.

It might also stop woke parents from becoming overly invested in the current transgender trend, which often gives them identity by proxy. Many gender activists become shrill at this point in the debate, but it's true.

And of course, while you should treat people with respect, the government has no right to tell you what pronoun to use when referring to someone. Yes, trans people should be respected, but no more than anybody else. And not via the censorship of others.

As I've already said elsewhere, people should be free to use whatever language they like. If they're an asshole to trans people by deliberately misgendering them, then they're an asshole—but they're allowed to be an asshole! The government shouldn't punish them for it. If they're calling for violence against a person who is trans or a group of trans people based on their identity, then we have a different issue on our hands.

So, in essence, let's respect trans people as individuals the same way we would respect anyone else. But let's also protect young people from overzealous activists caught up in the wokeness of the day.

The trans issue is particularly interesting because it directly affects such an infinitesimally small fraction of the population. While that group of people is worthy of equality and protection, ask yourself why this topic is being relentlessly pushed so hard. Is it genuine concern or is it another excuse to virtue signal while telling us how to think and feel?

That's a topic for a whole other book, but you probably already know the answer.

ECONOMICS

Back in 1999, I interned at Comedy Central's *The Daily Show*, which was then hosted by a little-known comedian called Jon Stewart.

There I worked pretty long hours doing a string of crappy jobs as most internships are designed to do, such as buying gum for Dave Chappelle, getting a six-pack of O'Doul's alcohol-free beer for George Carlin, and picking up tacos for Stephen Colbert (these were the highlights).

The far less glamorous duties included bringing people their mail, cleaning up after a meeting, and doing other assorted grunt work, but I was young and passionate and thought that it might lead me down the path to all my other aspirations.

When the internship wrapped up six months later, I'd fully realized how not paying people for work is an absolutely ridiculous premise. (Not to brag, but on my days off I was a part-time video game salesman at Electronics Boutique in Long Island, New York. All the while living back at my parent's house and sleeping in my childhood bedroom. The true American dream, right?)

I don't regret the experience at all, but I did learn a little something, though perhaps not the thing that the progressives at *The Daily Show* would've wanted me to learn . . .

Twenty years later, the lessons from this internship remain one of the main reasons why I won't hire unpaid interns at *The Rubin Report*, despite getting generous offers from people all over the country. Quite frankly, I just don't think it's fair to recruit staff at zero cost when you can afford to pay them a semidecent salary, even if just for a few weeks.

Does this mean I support a federally enforced minimum wage of $15 an hour? Absolutely not.

When it comes to economic policy, the state should mind its own business and allow people to manage their finances with maximum control.

That includes me, you, and everyone else.

This classically liberal approach was summed up by one of my heroes, the eminent professor Thomas Sowell, when he said: "I have never understood why it is 'greed' to want to keep the money you've earned, but not greed to want to take somebody else's money."

From my perspective, we should all be free to make as much money as possible and, crucially, keep the majority of it. Not give it away to the ever-growing welfare state to be managed by pointless government bureaucrats.

Sure, we've gotta pay something to finance the roads and the sanitation and emergency services, but the way we're currently "relieved" of our hard-earned money ought to be a crime.

If I were in charge of the Treasury Department I'd start by trimming back the size of the government by about a third. I bet nobody except government bureaucrats cashing their checks would even have a clue that anything changed. The federal government has increasingly become a giant, monstrous albatross that's only getting fatter and more inefficient.

Let's go even further. I'd minimize what the government gets by reducing the federal tax rate to a flat 18 percent for everyone—including big earners—with just a tiny handful of exceptions: those who make under $50,000 could pay 7 percent tax, while anyone banking more than $5 million can contribute 20 percent. And for the really poor, say, less than $25,000 annually, they can get a free ride; zero tax.

Everyone pays the same, that 18 percent, except a tiny bit more for those at the top, along with a bit of relief for those at the bottom. In a perfect world I'd do the 18 percent tax across the board, but perhaps a classical liberal is just a guilty libertarian.

As it stands right now, the top 1 percent already pay 90 percent of the money generated through federal tax, while the lower

10 percent pay basically nothing—yet still we're told the rich need to pay more.

This is nothing but class warfare, which is good for votes, but bad for policy.

And if the rich must pay more, then how much more—and for how long? Answers on a postcard please. Why not increase the rate annually until they're eventually paying 100 percent tax? That'll really teach them not to be greedy.

This anticapitalist approach does little to encourage entrepreneurialism and most likely does the opposite. Once again, Thomas Sowell nailed it when he said: "No government of the left has done as much for the poor as capitalism has. Even when it comes to the redistribution of income, the left talks the talk but the free market walks the walk."

Part of the confusion over a $15 an hour minimum wage seems to be the misguided belief that every job should be able to sustain an adult and family. This is wrong. The truth is that many jobs, especially low-paying ones, are meant to be an entry into the workforce, not a long-term career choice.

Just think back to your first job for a second. Was it worth $15 an hour? Unlikely. But even if it was, should it be the government's job to determine that number, or the job of the business that hired you?

Of course, the ultimate irony of the $15 minimum-wage crew is that nobody is stopping any company from paying it right now. Instead, Nike moves factories to China for cheap labor and the CEO of Walmart, Doug McMillon, calls for $15 minimum wage even though he doesn't institute it at his own company. (A brilliant move, by the way, because if it was ever passed, the higher wages would crush small businesses—including Walmart's competition.)

Artificially enforcing higher wages for low-skilled workers always ends badly because it ushers in automation, which replaces people with computers. Just look at McDonald's, where many cashiers have now been replaced by iPads. They've gone from low wage to no wage, which neatly takes me on to Social Security . . .

Yes, some type of safety net is good for those who need it most, but it should be a short-term gap. Not a long-term lifestyle.

Surely it would be better if our social programs operated on a limited amount of decreasing payments over a set time. This would encourage people to get back into the marketplace, rather than relinquishing their responsibility and giving up.

Right now the incentive structure is so out of whack that people who are fit to work eventually move over to long-term disability and never get off the government dole. In most cases I don't blame them; they're just taking advantage of a terrible system. But even putting aside who should receive welfare, how much they should receive, and for how long, we have a bigger problem on our hands. We simply can't afford any of it.

According to the Congressional Budget Office, the United States owes $22 trillion in debt—the highest it has ever been. This is absolutely bananas given that we're also the world's largest economy.

By 2029, our federal deficits—when Congress spends more than it raises through tax—are estimated to be $1.2 trillion every year.

Do the math. If the United States were a person, his or her credit cards would've been canceled already. So if you couldn't get away with it as an individual, then why should the government?

Instead of focusing on what we can have for "free," or on who we can take from to fund trendy, idealistic projects like the Green New Deal, let's focus on keeping what we earn and cutting spending wherever possible.

Remember when you were in fifth grade and your parents told you to save up for that bike you wanted? And how, after a couple months, you eventually saved enough money and got it?

Yeah, let's operate like that.

FOREIGN POLICY

When it comes to foreign policy, we need a strong military. Period.

This is simply the best way to achieve peace. It may sound like an oxymoron, but it's very much in line with President Ronald Reagan's "Peace through Strength" Cold War strategy.

People think that just because you're for a strong military it means that you're pro-war. But, actually, it's quite the opposite. I want our military to be universally feared so that we *don't* engage in more conflict.

This back-to-front logic is technically known as reverse psychology, which is a term coined by German philosopher Theodor Adorno and Max Horkheimer, back in 1970.

Their idea was that you can achieve a desired outcome by being counterintuitive and suggesting the opposite. In terms of war, this means the mere threat of military action can keep your adversaries in check.

So by being prepared to unleash force as a last resort, we actually end up promoting peace. Ironic, I know. But see how it works?

Progressives love to confuse this tactic with being trigger-happy— as if it's a display of our "toxic masculinity" or something—but they simply don't get it. It's the only realistic way for us to negotiate effectively in a dangerous world. But there's a catch . . .

It only works if our threat is credible.

This is why the worst foreign policy blunder of the last decade was arguably when Barack Obama implemented a red line in Syria, but did nothing when the Syrian government unleashed a chemical weapons attack.

"We have been very clear to the Assad regime, but also to other players on the ground, that a red line for us is seeing a whole bunch of chemical weapons moving around or being utilized," Obama said in August 2012. "That would change my calculus. That would change my equation."

A year later, in August 2013, the Ghouta chemical assault killed an estimated fifteen hundred people, including countless children who were pictured dead alongside their parents.

Obama's response? "I didn't set a red line."

Oh. OK then. Move along, there's nothing to see here . . .

Not only did this failure embolden our enemies, but our allies must've thought we'd lost our nerve. From their perspective, America's word was meaningless and we lacked the courage of our convictions. Suddenly we became a paper tiger. We looked scary, but a stiff wind could knock us over.

For the record, I always opposed intervention in Syria (and there are plenty of old YouTube videos that show me saying this on *The Young Turks*). I felt that after the disaster of Iraq it was time for some of the other regional actors to step up and do something to stabilize Syria, most notably Turkey or Saudi Arabia.

Once we'd committed to doing something, however, we had to back it up with action.

Preventive threats in other situations have been successful for years, which is why we cannot operate on a no-war policy.

Interestingly, Donald Trump has been resetting our policy of credible deterrence quite well. When he killed Iranian general Qasem Soleimani in an airstrike in January of 2020, many media elites and Twitter warriors proclaimed this was the beginning of World War III. As of this writing, the war has yet to break out. Bad news for MSNBC, good news for the rest of the world.

Bernie Sanders and his socialist buddies love to say that they'd avoid military action at all costs, but they ignore the fact that we're the world's last remaining superpower.

Does Bernie know that if we constantly say we are anti-war that it might actually bring war upon us? Perhaps he should try taking a Psych 101 class once he makes college free for everyone, including old socialists.

The point is, if we don't assert ourselves in the face of tyranny, who will? It certainly won't be international alliances like NATO. Just look at what happened to Ukraine. It gave up its nukes to become a NATO country (which guarantees protection to all subscribed nations if attacked), but when Russia invaded Crimea, Ukraine got zero support. The country gave up its most potent weapons for a signed bit of paper, which meant absolutely nothing. Think Ukraine regrets that now?

The same goes for France and the United Kingdom. They're two of the most staunch allies of America, but they're not gonna save the world when the next genocide comes knocking. Ultimately, that duty falls on us.

A quick glance through history proves this: we defeated the Nazis and the Japanese imperialists, and most recently made a huge dent on ISIS, which is a reminder that the world is at its safest when America is strongest.

And unless we have a decent foreign policy, we are not strong. We're vulnerable.

Therefore, we must have a robust defense, protect our borders, build good relationships with like-minded allies, and encourage global democracy through nonmilitary means.

Whether it's self-serving or not, this includes drawing back our presence from countries such as Germany and Japan (which, by the way, don't pay us to defend them) and withdrawing our troops from Afghanistan, a country with which we've now been in the longest-running war in U.S. history.

Yes, that's right. Afghanistan is now the longest war we've ever been in. It's gone on for so long that it barely even gets any media attention at all.

Instead, if we want to support democratic leaders in other countries, we should do it through education and the spread of ideas, not by toppling regimes like former U.S. president George W. Bush did in Iraq.

It is also what Obama did when we attacked Libya with his "kinetic military action"—a move that wasn't even approved by Congress. This "action" ended up being such a colossal failure that what's left of Libya remains a barely functioning country.

Yeah, he brought down Colonel Gaddafi, who was a brutal dictator to say the least, but things ended up being worse off. Instead of becoming a democracy, it's now a failed state in which violent deaths are commonplace, rival militias fight for power, and the Islamic State group (ISIS) has influence.

Regardless of your political affiliation, there's no way this can be considered a success story for U.S. foreign policy. Even Obama has described it as his "worst mistake" while in office. Let's not repeat this!

A sane foreign policy protects our homeland, enhances relationships with democratic allies, helps spread the ideas of human freedom, and uses its military might only when absolutely necessary.

This concept is not imperialist, nor pacifist. It is realist.

So there you have it. These are my takes based on a truly liberal perspective.

Simply because you've chosen to read this book, I doubt you're offended, crying, or literally shaking. But you might disagree. Maybe you're a pro-life Christian, or a conservative who has a different position on abortion than I do. If that's the case, good! Clapback. Gather the facts and email them to me. Start a conversation with someone from a different ideological background.

The point of this chapter is not to tell you how to think. It's to show you how to calmly, respectfully, and confidently defend yourself. Because defending the truth is the right thing to do—and it's the attitude that animates safe and free societies.

I know what you're thinking: but people aren't respectful to me, so why should I extend them such courtesy?

Unfortunately, you're right that people often become condescending and out of line when you're brave enough to represent the facts no matter where they lead. They resort to insulting your character instead of challenging your ideas.

In the next chapter, I'll show you how to survive and thrive when they decide you're the enemy.

4

Don't Worry, You're Not a Nazi

CONGRATULATIONS, I HAVE fantastic news—you are *not* a Nazi!

You may be wondering how I know this, considering we've probably never met, but trust me, I know. What's vital going forward is that you know this too.

See, we live in strange times. Very strange times. An era in which people secretly hope you are a Nazi, because then at least they'd have a real villain to rage against.

Unfortunately for them, supply doesn't meet demand, so they frequently turn to political gaslighting: a form of psychological manipulation that makes its targets second-guess themselves.

This tactic can manifest in various ways, but the result is always the same. By the end you're so confused that you question everything about yourself—even whether you're a secret extremist who goose-steps while asleep.

So let me say it one more time for the record: you are not a Nazi. Let's look at the evidence.

Exhibit A: I'm guessing you're no fan of socialism, which was a founding principle of the Nazi movement. The name "Nazi" is an acronym for the National Socialist German Workers' Party, which most of today's Democrat socialists conveniently forget. Actually, that's an understatement. These people don't just overlook this truth, they've totally rewritten history on the matter.

These days, Nazism gets associated with conservatism at the drop of a hat, but historically it stems from the left. Adolf Hitler? An art-loving vegetarian who seized power by wooing voters away from Germany's Social Democrat and communist parties.

Italy's Benito Mussolini? Raised on Karl Marx's *Das Kapital* before starting his career as a left-wing journalist and, later, implementing a deadly fascist regime.

Exhibit B: Real Nazis hated gays and Jews to the point of mass extermination of them in purpose-built death camps, so it's pretty unlikely that I would suddenly be their go-to choice for bedtime reading, even if this is a page-turner.

Exhibit C: You've just paid about $20 to learn my take on classical liberalism—an ideology that, if fashionable back in 1930s Germany, might've stopped the Third Reich before it even started. See, classical liberals oppose judging people based on ethnicity or religion. They only judge the individual. They'd also never want to hand so much power over to the government. Therefore, any modern-day Nazi worth his salt would be burning this book, not thumbing through it. (Though if you do burn this book, please take a picture of it and use hashtag #DONTBURNTHISBOOK on Instagram.)

So relax, you're not a Nazi. Oh, and you're also not "literally Hitler," because he's dead. Mazel tov!

This may seem like a strange way to start a chapter, and I'd be inclined to agree, but it's worth driving home in today's nutty political climate. See, these days, any reasonable person who entertains a conservative principle—even something as mundane as small government or low taxes—can be linked to the amorphous far right, which is quite a reach. Even for progressives.

The psychology behind this leap is as follows: if you're a sane person, progressives would need to consider your views like reasonable adults. But because they don't want to question their narrow, dogmatic worldview, they categorize you as extreme. This enables them to completely dismiss you without feeling bad. In fact, it makes them feel morally righteous. In their minds they've exterminated a deadly enemy.

Here's a random sample from my own experiences . . .

Not long ago I was branded "a [Nazi] fascist disguised in the skin/clothes/tones of a *Today Show* correspondent," which I found particularly outrageous. After all, I dress way better than anyone on NBC's morning schedule.

Another said: "Dave Rubin isn't *technically* a Nazi, but he's definitely a collaborator and there's no meaningful functional difference at this point," which was really eye-opening for me. Then, a third declared: "[He] isn't a Nazi. It's just that he'd sit across from Himmler and say 'interesting' a lot."

Fortunately, this all happened in the alternative reality of Twitter, where such things are posted by anonymous accounts with anime avatars. Sadly, the mainstream media is rarely any better.

After spending a full day in my home, where he was welcomed with open arms, journalist Philipp Oehmke described me as "the biggest illusionist associated with the alt-right movement" in a piece for *Der Spiegel* magazine.

On the surface, his life looks like that of a model progressive. He lives in a modernist house made of exposed concrete, glass and Scandinavian wood. Inside, an artist friend is at work on a painting on a large canvas. There are framed covers of the *New Yorker* on the wall in the foyer. This is where Rubin lives with his husband David, who is making coffee with an Italian coffee-maker. From a studio in his converted two-car garage, Rubin broadcasts his "Rubin Report," in which he, with affected gen-uine curiosity, often provides other alt-right figures with talking points in the form of suggestive questions.

OK, time for some basic fact-checking:

- There's no exposed concrete in my home, but this still wouldn't make me alt-right.
- The "artist friend" is actually my sister-in-law, Caylin Janet. She's an absolutely brilliant painter who has done most of the pieces in my home. She says hi.
- The Italian coffee maker is not a symbol of elitism. It's a basic Nespresso machine, which can be picked up from your local Target for $149. (Fun fact: I got mine from a cast member of *The Big Bang Theory* as a wedding gift.)
- Oh, and the wall of framed *New Yorkers*? That's one postcard, which I bought for literally $5 before leaving my beloved home city of Manhattan. But I digress . . .

"He has two Muslim guests on his show today," Oehmke continued:

> But it soon becomes apparent that the two guests, an Egyptian woman named Yasmine Mohammed and Faisal Said al-Mutar from Iraq, are ex-Muslims—and that they despise Islam.
>
> And while the entire setting suggests that this is an ordinary talk show, Rubin has Mohammed explain how bad Islam is. She claims that she was 'married to al-Qaeda' against her will. Mutar, the Iraqi, clearly enjoys the fact that for him, the normal boundaries of political correctness have been suspended and that he, as a hater of Islam, has a voice that right-wing America loves to hear.

Oehmke heavily implied that I'm somehow "Islamophobic," which seems more disturbing to him than Yasmine's arranged marriage or Faisal's brother being killed by jihadists. His assumptions about all of our intentions say far more about him than it does about us.

Furthermore, Yasmine and Faisal are not puppets. They have their own minds. Implying otherwise is pretty damn patronizing to them both.

"As a journalist, he could have easily looked up my 'claim' that I was married to a member of Al Qaeda," Mohammed later told me. "My ex-husband was involved in the largest terrorism court case in Egyptian history after the assassination of President Anwar Sadat. It would not be difficult to verify my 'claim.' But he had zero interest in the truth. He was only interested in confirming the narrative he arrived with. I was not a human being to him. I was simply a pawn in his game. [That interview on *The Rubin Report*] was the first time I felt validated. That I didn't feel like someone was talking over me and telling me what I thought. I will be forever grateful for that."

Unfortunately, around the same time, I was also slimed by "journalist" Josh Harkinson in a piece for *Mother Jones* titled "Cashing in on the Rise of the Alt-Right." This article also flirted with libel by claiming I was "far right" (read: shorthand for Nazi) because I had the temerity to interview people with different views. Truly hateful, I know.

It even went on to say that crowdfunded shows such as mine were "a new breed of extremist social and independent media," which, of course, is just jealous nonsense. My show is voluntarily financed by thousands of people across the political spectrum—including legitimately concerned members of the left, so nope, it's not bankrolled by the far right!

Oh, and as far as "cashing-in" goes, moving to the heavily progressive city of Los Angeles and going against the dominant, left-wing narrative is hardly a guaranteed road to riches.

Eventually, the editors at *Mother Jones* backpedaled, but only after I fought back and stared them down. It was an unpleasant wake-up call about media bias, but it illustrates my point. Now, simply interviewing ex-Muslims, being crowdfunded, or owning a coffee machine (!) is enough to be branded evil, even if you've spent your entire life on the left, like me.

I come from a liberal Jewish family in New York. Being open-minded and socially conscious is pretty much stamped onto my DNA. Being a Democrat was like a second religion to my parents' generation.

From a young age it was instilled in me that healthy conflict or having different views—the very premise of *The Rubin Report*—is a good thing. Actually, we were taught it was vital to personal and intellectual development. Every holiday involved sitting around a huge makeshift table and debating the latest hot-button issues: from abortion to the death penalty and Israel (it was more fun than it sounds, honest).

There's an old joke that if you have three Jews at a table, then you have four opinions. Now try a family of thirty! That was my home life and I truly loved the endless debate. But our differences never surpassed our respect for one another. By the time dessert was done we'd pressed the reset button and let it all go.

It was a playful battle of ideas. It was also the original safe space because there was no punishment for having an "incorrect" view—well, apart from the time my aunt claimed that the *Friends* sitcom was funnier than *Seinfeld*, which almost split the family apart.

Naively, as I grew up, finished school, and graduated from college, I'd hoped to have the same understanding with my peers in the real world. But, obviously, that has not been the case for me or many of the guests on my show.

Back in 2016, conservative commentator Ben Shapiro was speaking at college campuses across the United States. As an Orthodox Jew, complete with the yarmulke, he's clearly no fan of Hitler—but a full-scale riot erupted when he appeared at California State University. Hundreds of students protested his presence, and the threat of violence was so serious that armed police were drafted in to help control the madness.

It later transpired that one of the professors had told her students that he was a "Nazi," which is totally insane given Shapiro lost several relatives from his father's side in the Holocaust.

Like most other Jews, my own family has a tragic history related to World War II . . .

My uncle's father, Joseph Berger, suffered a horrendous fate after *real* Nazis invaded his native Poland in 1939. Along with his wife and their two young daughters, Janina and Celina, they were rounded up and forced to relocate to a squalid ghetto with three hundred thousand other Jews, a space roughly ten blocks wide, with a crude perimeter fence manned by armed SS guards. Tuberculosis and other diseases were rife. Dead bodies of men, women, and children littered the compound.

Luckily, Joseph was allowed to work at his day job in a lumberyard, and as the ghetto conditions worsened, he bribed a local businessman into building a makeshift annex at the back of the company warehouse. Here, the family would live undercover until the war was over. At least that was the master plan . . .

Days before going into hiding, the setup changed. The businessman behind it refused to take Celina, who was then just three years old, because she was too young. He feared her crying might blow their cover and they'd all be murdered.

Panicked, Joseph was forced to hatch a new, hugely ambitious plan, which meant brainwashing his daughter into believing she was not a Jew but a gentile called Mary. After weeks of brainwashing, he succeeded, and then, against all his paternal instincts, abandoned her in the local park of a Christian neighborhood, where he hoped somebody—anybody—would find and adopt her.

Days later, Joseph was packed onto a cattle train and sent to

Buchenwald concentration camp, where he was stripped, shaved, and tattooed with his prisoner number: 86969.

Soon after, he learned that his wife and eldest daughter had been shot dead.

Devastated, he somehow escaped the camp while working off-site, but was shot twice in the leg by guards. After months of living in the wild as a fugitive, he was finally liberated by the Russians.

Suddenly free, he immediately began the long and desperate search for his only surviving daughter. He eventually tracked her down to a monastery in the mountains.

There, Joseph found "Mary" collecting firewood, but she didn't recognize him. It had been too long. When staff refused to believe they were related, he kidnapped her.

He returned at night, climbed the six-foot fence, and put a chloroform rag over her face as she slept. He then threw her into the back of a truck and drove away.

Finally, they were reunited, but they were also complete strangers.

It took years of pain before they had anything that resembled a good relationship. The scars of that time reverberated throughout all of their lives and even into the generations that came after them.

Yet, with total disrespect for such horrifying lived experiences, which involved real Nazis—as opposed to the ones people imagine—the media's far-right inference continues.

In March 2019, *The Economist*—a center-right, respectable publication based in London—ran an in-depth article on Shapiro that called him "a pop idol of the alt right." Yet again, editors were forced to retract their comments and publicly apologize, but only after he went on a Twitter rampage and forced them to do their job responsibly.

Then, in the same month, noted feminist Christina Hoff Sommers was branded "white supremacy-adjacent" by feminist Roxane Gay. Her reasoning? That our beloved "Based Mom" once appeared at an event with Milo Yiannopoulos and didn't disavow him enough.

That's right, people, fascism is contagious and spreads by proxy! Merely being next to somebody, who's next to somebody else, makes them a Nazi. Unfortunately, it seems Ms. Gay hadn't thought this one through, because—by her own reasoning—simply appearing at an event with Christina makes her white supremacy-adjacent too. Awkward!

Days later, the mob then went after my friend (and—shock, horror!—black conservative) Candace Owens during a House Judiciary Committee on hate crimes. There, she was deliberately misrepresented as a Hitler apologist by Democrat congressman Ted Lieu.

He knowingly took a ten-second clip from a six-minute speech and tried to frame her as a bigot, while her seventy-five-year-old grandfather, who once picked cotton in North Carolina, sat right behind her. Classy.

Unlike Lieu, I know Owens personally. I've appeared on her show and she's been on mine. We've had dinners at my house, I attended her wedding, and we've knocked back plenty of frozen margaritas together. Believe me, this wouldn't have happened if she was an anti-Semite (I only drink light beer with anti-Semites and she only drinks IPAs with racists).

Then of course there's Jordan Peterson, who's perhaps the most maligned of all.

There are endless examples of him being referred to as a "dog whistle" for white supremacists and "angry, straight men," but the madness culminated when his critically acclaimed book, *12 Rules for Life: An Antidote to Chaos*, was pulled from bookstores in New Zealand after the massacre of fifty people in two Christchurch mosques. Although it wasn't explicitly stated, the insinuation was that he was somehow responsible for the shootings after being pictured with a random fan during a meet and greet.

The person in question, who was literally among thousands to be photographed backstage, was wearing a T-shirt that read *I'm a proud Islamaphobe.* When the picture appeared online, Peterson's offer for a visiting fellowship at Cambridge University was withdrawn. Weirdly enough, mainstream outlets didn't bother to mention the full text printed on the shirt, which denounced the mistreatment of women and gays.

Although Peterson wasn't endorsing the fan's crude message—jeez, he probably didn't even read the damn thing—the "new gestapo" concluded that this one image was conclusive proof of his far-right motives. It was guilt by association, which is seriously bad news for Oprah Winfrey and Meryl Streep, who've both been photographed with Harvey Weinstein.

Meanwhile, back in the real world, politicians such as Ilhan Omar can be blatantly anti-Semitic, implying that Jews have dual loyalty, *which is literally what Hitler said*—yet progressives give her a free pass. Nancy Pelosi, speaker of the House of Representatives, even defended Omar's bile, saying: "I don't think our colleague is anti-Semitic. I think she has a different experience in the use of words."

This is a prime example of the left's soft bigotry of low expectations.

Omar, a Somali immigrant, may be smart enough to be on the

House Foreign Relations Committee, but she's apparently too dumb to use the English language properly.

In other words: when it's convenient she's black, female, and Muslim—all things that score big in the Oppression Olympics—yet, when the mask slips and her ideas require scrutiny, she's immediately protected via the victimhood status that comes with those labels. It's quite a brilliant strategy, actually. Play the victim card to attain power, then, once you have it, use it to shield yourself from legitimate criticism.

This cognitive dissonance stems from one key truth about modern leftism: progressives see racism, sexism, and discrimination everywhere, *except where it actually exists.*

That's not to say America doesn't have issues with prejudice and discrimination. Do white supremacists exist? Yes. Do black, Jew, and Hispanic haters exist? Yes. But are these people fringe and irrelevant? Hell yeah. They have no institutional power. And that's exactly how it should be.

There is a huge, monumental difference between this sort of behavior and acknowledging facts that contradict the left's narrative. Let me explain in really patronizing detail . . .

Think America should be a white ethnostate? Sorry, but you're a racist. It goes against the very founding principles of America, which say that "there is no natural class of rulers among people, and everyone is born with the same unalienable rights to life, liberty, and the pursuit of happiness."

Has America always succeeded at this? Unfortunately not. But it's always worked hard to do better. And it's still doing that now.

That being said, it's still not racist to observe that half of the homicides in America are committed by and against African Americans. There may be countless reasons behind this, and I truly wish things were different, but it's a fact. This is not racist. If anything, it's racist to ignore this and make the task of finding a solution even more difficult.

The same principle applies to every other social group, including women.

Think men are inherently better solely because of their birth gender? Unless we're talking about the ability to pee standing up, you're probably sexist.

Recognizing that biological differences exist between the genders does *not,* however, make you misogynistic. I'm living proof of this. I love my mother, who's a woman. I also love my sister, who's another woman. Plus, I named my car Dorothy Zbornak after Bea Arthur's character in *The Golden Girls* sitcom (and one of my pet chickens is called Blanche Featheraux . . . in honor of Rue McClanahan). No hatred of women here!

In fact, it probably makes me *more* supportive of women when I don't take pleasure in watching male-to-female trans athletes pummel girls in wrestling matches.

That said, I can also respect the transgender community without wanting my language and pronoun usage to be dictated by the state.

I once made this explicitly clear during an appearance at the University of New Hampshire. There, while being heckled by a trans protester, I calmly asserted that I wanted her to be treated with dignity and respect under the law, which is the same thing I would want for anyone else. I also deliberately used her preferred pronouns out of respect, despite the fact she didn't show me any in return.

It turned out that she was a gender studies professor at the university. Yes, you got that right: a professor at a university using her right to free speech to shut down an invited speaker.

Amazingly, this sort of emotional outburst is becoming more and more common within the LGBT world.

The Advocate's treatment of openly gay tech maven Peter Thiel was another case of the left's cancel culture. Some of its adherents blackballed him from the LGBT community for his support of Donald Trump (who's also not a Nazi, even if you despise him).

Their article titled "Peter Thiel Shows Us There's a Difference between Gay Sex and Gay" was wildly homophobic, but the editors— who were once pioneers of the gay civil rights movement—couldn't see this beyond their own agenda.

"This intolerance has taken on some bizarre forms," Thiel later hit back in a speech at the National Press Club. "*The Advocate*, a magazine which once praised me as a 'gay innovator,' published an article saying that as of now I am, and I quote, 'not a gay man,' because I don't agree with their politics.

"The lie behind the buzzword of 'diversity' could not be made more clear: if you don't conform, then you don't count as 'diverse,' no matter what your personal background."

And Thiel is absolutely correct. If anything, it is members of the hard-line left who are the new radicals to fear. I'm not saying every single one of them is bad. I know there are many good lefties who share my concerns. As you might guess, I'm writing this for them too. But I truly believe it's the far-left puritans who are the greatest threat to our free, pluralistic democracy.

The left's obsession with identity politics is the reverse of the melting-pot principle that America was founded upon: a place where everyone, regardless of race, religion, and color, is welcome as long as they blend into the fabric of our (free) society.

The left's obsession with judging us on immutable characteristics is what will eventually reach a tipping point and turn neighbor against neighbor, dividing America . . . and beyond.

It's progressive activists who are banning people from having bank accounts, from speaking at universities, and from social media platforms and crowdfunding sites. They have huge influence over the media and the political lobby. Their modus operandi has chilling parallels to the tactics seen in 1940s Germany, which is also technically cultural appropriation. No kidding. They've literally taken the horrific, archaic ideas of the past and imported them into the here and now. This is true cultural appropriation, not whether you have dreadlocks or wear hoop earrings.

My point? The left's nonstop, casual use of the term *Nazi* to shame, defame, and besmirch is so indiscriminate, so scattergun, and so preposterous that you're almost duty bound to disregard it.

Once you understand this, you can laugh at it, which is the greatest weapon against the new N-word. You're not a Nazi, you're just somebody who thinks for themselves.

If you appreciate this on a deep, cellular level, the term *Nazi* and all its radioactive implications won't hold sway over you. It won't make you insecure in your opinions.

You'll never need to question your motivation because it'll be built on a solid understanding that's unshakable, like the granite that underpins the skyscrapers of Manhattan.

Now that your foundation is reinforced, it's time to start building.

5

Check Your Facts, Not Your Privilege

THE BEST AND WORST moment of my career happened at exactly the same time.

It was January 2016 and came during an interview with conservative radio host Larry Elder, who was making his first appearance on *The Rubin Report*.

Elder, the self-described "Sage of South Central," had long been challenging the progressive narrative as an outspoken black conservative. And he was fearless about it.

The son of a janitor who was raised in a working-class home, he was living proof that race and class don't hold people back. He did this by becoming a bestselling author (several times over) and hosting the longest-running drive time radio show in Los Angeles.

Prior to his appearance, most of my guests had been liberals such as Sam Harris, Gad Saad, Maajid Nawaz (who coined the term *regressive left*), and Peter Boghossian, who'd also started to recognize the left's issues.

Looking back, this was more like group therapy for liberals who were just catching on to the new woke progressives. Each week

I became more confident in my beliefs because I realized that there were smart, decent people all over the world who were having the same frustrations as I was.

Elder was the first conservative figure I would interview, and from the very beginning, he meant business. After years of having to defend himself against left-leaning TV anchors, such as CNN's Don Lemon and Wolf Blitzer, the man knew how to win a debate.

I thought I did too, because I'd inadvertently surrounded myself with people who (for the most part) agreed with me. Sure, I was dipping my toe into new political waters with each episode of the show, but I never truly had my views challenged—at least not aggressively. Boy, was that about to change . . .

Although I was prepared on one level—as the host asking all the questions—nothing could have prepared me for the red pill that Larry was going to put into my mouth and force me to swallow.

Worse yet, millions of people all over the internet were going to watch me gag as it went down. Now there's a sentence I never thought I'd write!

I opened the interview with a joke about the elephant in the room. "I'm gonna look at my notes, but apparently you're black?" I said.

"Yep, that's correct," he replied, laughing. "I'm black—not African American. That's a term I don't like. I was born in America and I've never been to Africa. It's an absurd term. A term that Jesse Jackson crammed down the throats of the media. It's ridiculous."

My alarm bell should've gone off here. The man was a trained lawyer who'd been steelmanning his position for decades and successfully taking unpopular positions against the progressive agenda.

For example, he loved to dismantle the commonly held idea

that high unemployment rates among the black population are due to widespread discrimination, hiring biases, and laws that impose workplace barriers.

If I'd challenged my own beliefs sooner, I might've recognized this.

Leftism, however, was still strongly running through my veins, so I was blind to my own ignorance. It all became painfully obvious when I asked him about "systemic racism" in America—a social theory I presented as fact.

"Give me an example," he said, cutting me off. "Tell me what you think the most systemic issue is."

Cue: the biggest defining moment of my professional life.

No guest had ever turned a question like this right back at me—and I didn't know where to start. Surely it wasn't my job as an interviewer to defend my position. Isn't that the guest's responsibility? This suddenly was becoming a bizarro-land interview.

Flummoxed, all I could do was regurgitate the preprogrammed talking points that were lodged into my brain from years of osmosis.

First, I brought up the issue of slavery. "Well, er, I would say . . . because black people . . . in most cases, err, were descendants of slaves that racism . . . er . . . it just exists," I said, throwing a few random buzzwords into a semicoherent sentence.

Larry wasn't convinced. "What's your basis for saying that?" he hit back, continuing the reversal of our roles as interviewer/ interviewee. "Give me an example. Tell me what you think the most systemic racist issue is. What is it?"

Once again, I relied on the "wisdom" of my factory settings. "I think you could probably find evidence that, in general, cops are . . . er, more willing to shoot if the, er, perpetrator, is . . . black?"

Nope. I still wasn't gaining ground on him.

"What's your data? What's your basis for saying that?" Larry challenged. "Nine hundred and sixty-five people were shot by cops [in 2015]. [Only] four percent of them were white cops shooting unarmed blacks. Half the homicides in this country are committed by (and against) black people. Last year there were fourteen thousand homicides. Ninety-six percent of them were black-on-black. Where are the Black Lives Matter people on that?"

He added: "In Chicago, in 2011, twenty-one [black] people were shot and killed by [white] cops. In 2015 there were [just] seven. [Chicago's population] is a third black, a third white, and a third Hispanic, yet seventy percent of the homicides are black-on-black, so the idea that a racist white cop is a peril to black people is total BS."

Oh man, I've really stepped in it now, I thought. *Could these numbers be true? And, if they were, why hadn't I been briefed? Was this breaking news or something? For God's sake, somebody tell the ladies of* The View.

This was a bloodbath and I was the one being bludgeoned.

It got particularly painful when Elder brought up the death of Freddie Gray, a Baltimore man who'd died in the back of a police van ten months earlier. The default position of virtually everyone in mainstream media and the online world, including myself, had chalked it up to another example of systemic racism. But not Larry.

"[Baltimore] is a city that's forty-five percent black," he said unapologetically.

"The city council is one hundred percent Democrat. The majority of the city council is black. The top cop at the time was black. The number two cop was black. The majority of the command staff was black. The mayor is black. The attorney general is black. And yet here we are talking about racism? It's absurd."

I remember feeling physically uncomfortable in my chair as Larry laid out the incontrovertible truth. I'd lost control of the interview and had to grab it back . . . somehow.

In order to do this, I shamefully played the "liberal hero" card. "It's funny, I find myself caught in the middle," I said. "As a liberal, I always want to try and defend others—in this case, blacks. I'm always sympathetic to that."

Even though I didn't realize it, this was a cop-out lefties almost always use when confronted with reality. Sure, he just laid out a ton of stats that disprove my original position, but hey, I'm still a liberal, a good guy, so cut me some slack.

But he *still* wouldn't let up.

"I asked you to name the most important example of racism," he said. "You gave me white cops going after black people, but I already gave you the facts on that. I need some specifics. You're the one who made the assertion that racism remains a major problem in America. You didn't hold it up very well, so what's the other argument you have? I'm not mad, I just wanna know what you're talking about."

Elder was right and he damn well knew it.

"The biggest burden that black people have is being raised without fathers," he declared. "A black kid raised without a dad is five times more likely to be poor and commit crime, nine times more likely to drop out of school, and twenty times more likely to end up in jail. When I hear people tell me about systemic racism or unconscious racism I always say 'give me an example.' And almost nobody can do it. I give the facts . . . and [according to left-wingers] the facts are racist."

Now he really had me. Saying that a family is better off with a father shouldn't be controversial and it certainly isn't racist. But my side, the left, had made it both.

According to talkpoverty.org, a project of the Center for American Progress, the media narrative around two-parent families "is racist and homophobic. It needs to stop."

Meanwhile, sociology professor Jessie Daniels from New York's City University claimed that "the white nuclear family is one of the most powerful forces supporting white supremacy."

She went on to argue that "forming a white family" and having "white children" perpetuates racism and is "part of the problem."

This is interesting, considering that it completely contradicts the facts.

As Walter E. Williams, a professor of economics from George Mason University, has previously said, the biggest problem among blacks is actually the weak family structure—not white people daring to procreate.

As he noted in *The Daily Signal*, children from fatherless homes are likelier to drop out of high school, die by suicide, have behavioral disorders, join gangs, commit crimes, and end up in prison. They are also more likely to live in poverty-stricken households.

Conversely, nuclear families—whether black or white—are richer in all ways.

"Two-parent black families are rarely poor," he said in 2017. "Only eight percent of black married-couple families live in poverty. Among black families in which both the husband and wife work full time, the poverty rate is under five percent.

"Poverty in black families headed by single women is thirty-seven percent. The undeniable truth is that neither slavery nor Jim Crow nor the harshest racism has decimated the black family the way the welfare state has. The black family structure is not the only retrogression suffered by blacks in the age of racial enlightenment."

Deep down, I knew the importance of an intact family. I think we all do. Yet here I was, a good liberal from a two-parent home, scared of speaking the truth for fear of being called racist.

I didn't just know this intellectually, I'd lived it. I grew up in a stable home in Long Island with my parents, younger brother, and sister, riding my bike around town or playing the latest Nintendo video games. There were no family breakups, no drug use, no physical or psychological abuse—which is pretty good going considering we lived just thirty miles from 1980s Manhattan.

Sure, it wasn't a perfect existence. We had family drama just like everyone else. But we also had stability, both emotionally and financially. This isn't to say there aren't successful single parents out there, but let's face it: nothing trumps the nuclear family when it comes to offering the best possible starting point in life. This is a time-tested theory that has manifested itself in every part of the world throughout the ages.

Yet back in the studio with Elder, I was scared to admit it.

When the interview finally wrapped, Larry and I shook hands before we parted ways. At this point I remember cringing, hard. I remember being too embarrassed to even look the cameramen in the eye because they'd witnessed my intellectual execution firsthand.

"Don't worry, we'll cut that bit out," one of the producers said as I entered the control room. But I didn't hesitate in telling him that it had to air in full. No cuts.

To be crystal clear: everything that happened during this interview was totally my fault. Elder owned me and I deserved it. Before then, like so many of my peers on the left, I'd assumed there was only one answer to society's ills—and that it was to be found on my team's side of the court. This wasn't a well-thought-out political position, but it's the one I'd held until this eye-opening conversation.

My thinking was that Elder had won fair and square and I needed to honor his victory, no matter how uncomfortable. Plus, whether I liked it or not, this devastatingly embarrassing moment was everything *The Rubin Report* was meant to be about—pushing personal and political growth through conversation.

Think about just how shortsighted and doggedly partisan the news media is today. Turn on any political TV show and you'll see a conservative defending his or her position in the face of accusations from a progressive "good guy." By putting my pride aside, we were able to do something that is so rarely done on TV or even online. We could show that people actually do grow and change when confronted with reality.

Days later, when the clips went viral, I felt a renewed wave of humiliation. There was a steady stream of memes and GIFs, each more biting than the last, with captions featuring the obligatory uppercase verbs—"Elder DESTROYS Rubin," "Hero DEMOLISHES lefty snowflake," etc.

This was the first time I wasn't thrilled that my name was associated with a video counting millions of views. I felt I had done the right thing, but I couldn't avoid the embarrassment that came along with it. I wanted to run and hide, but where would I go? My only option was to embrace it all, which I did.

Normally, I would never recommend reading the comments section of YouTube videos, but in this case, I'm glad I did. After I got over my bad feelings, I noticed people were actually with me.

"You can tell he's just floored by the amount of knowledge and stats he was blind too [*sic*]," said one. "Props to Dave for learning and changing his opinions instead of ignoring and falling back into that [liberal] bubble."

Another added: "Wow, as a liberal myself, I can honestly say that I was taken on a journey with this interview. There really is a 'penny dropped' moment here for Dave. I felt it myself."

This made me realize that losing a debate isn't a sign of stupidity or weakness, but a sign of growth *if you're willing to embrace it with humility*.

I was reminded of this two years later when we shot *The Rubin Report* with the legendary economist and author Dr. Thomas Sowell while on location at Stanford University in April 2018. Sowell is a conservative who just so happens to be black, as well as a mentor to Elder, so it felt like the perfect opportunity to acknowledge the lesson I'd learned—and reaffirm it once more.

So when I asked him what caused his own transition from far-left Marxist to modern-day libertarian, his answer was perfectly summarized when he simply quipped: "Facts."

His observation is absolutely correct. But there's a reason people like Sowell—thoughtful conservatives whose positions are supported by obvious facts—are misunderstood and even demonized by the left. Political dialogue isn't as simple as a mutual presentation of facts. It's often a conflict of political languages. If one person speaks the language of conservatives and the other speaks the language of progressives, the chances that they will engage with each other on the level of facts are low. I can see how I found it difficult to listen simply because of his conservative worldview.

Arnold Kling's book *The Three Languages of Politics* explains this best. In it, Kling argues that political discourse is dysfunctional because people speak different political languages—and it's impossible to communicate or understand someone who's speaking in a completely different tongue. Once you become aware of which language you speak, you'll not only be more mindful of your own ideological commitments, but you'll also be able to better understand how your political opponents view the world.

Kling identifies three primary languages:

- Liberals see the world as a battle between victims and oppressors.
- Conservatives see the world as a battle between civilization and barbarism.
- Libertarians see the world as a battle between liberty and coercion.

For clarity's sake, Kling's "liberals" are progressives—American twenty-first-century liberals, not classical liberals. So if you're a progressive liberal, you see America and the West in general as an oppressive, tyrannical regime bent on capitalist destruction and oppression.

Conservatives, who generally view the world through more of a religious lens, want to maintain the hard-fought freedoms we have (civilization) while protecting them from the whims of the day (barbarism). Meanwhile, libertarians see big government and the political machine as the biggest threat to personal freedom.

Kling's point is that no matter what language we speak, we should use slow thinking, not fast thinking. Citing Daniel Kahneman's bestselling book *Thinking, Fast and Slow*, Kling argues that we go wrong in political discourse when we hear a fact in isolation and jump to conclusions without considering its context. He encourages us to consider political problems slowly and logically instead—much like Elder did in our 2016 interview.

I would also add to this that, at times, each of these lenses is more effective and needed than at other times. I find the classical liberal view to be the most encompassing of all three lenses, positing a defense of victims over oppressors, a defense of civilization over barbarism, and a promise of freedom over coercion.

In the rest of this chapter, I'm going to give you some of the most important data points on several of today's most pressing issues—but I'm also going to show you how to consider their context before jumping to conclusions.

Of course, the following is not designed to be exhaustive. Instead, it's here to make you think. And to set you on the path to learn more for yourself. There are dozens if not hundreds of books written about each of these topics, and if you're interested, you should explore some of them. Perhaps even find some that go against what I've laid out here, and see what you think.

So, with that in mind, here's a guide to some surprising facts on today's big issues, including gun control, the so-called wage gap, hate crimes, and the (two) genders.

Grab your therapy dog, stock up on Xanax, and take a deep breath. We're going in . . .

SYSTEMIC RACISM

Great news for everyone except progressives—we are less racist than ever before!

That's according to the General Social Survey (GSS), which is run by the University of Chicago's National Opinion Research Center.

GSS repeatedly quizzed a vast sample of people with the same questions from 1972 onward and found a steady move toward tolerance. Initially, 15 percent of white respondents thought "black and white children should go to separate public schools." That figure dropped to 10 percent in the early 1980s and became a negligible amount by 1985—so much so that GSS stopped asking the question.

Similarly, 65 percent of white people opposed interracial marriages in 1990, but that dropped to 25 percent by 2008.

A more recent study, conducted by Harvard University's Tessa Charlesworth and Mahzarin Banaji, is even more reassuring. It found both conscious and unconscious racial bias had "declined significantly" between 2007 and 2016. They studied 4.4 million online tests from across the United States over thirteen years and concluded: "Even within just a decade, all explicit responses showed change toward attitude neutrality."

Black people are 23.5 percent *less* likely to be shot by police, relative to whites. That's according to ex-Harvard scholar Roland Fryer (a black dude, I might add). He investigated racial profiling in his study: "An Empirical Analysis of Racial Differences in Police Use of Force," published July 2017.

A year earlier, a Washington State University paper ("The Reverse Racism Effect," written by Lois James, Stephen M. James, and Bryan J. Vila, and published in the May 2016 *Criminology & Public Policy* journal), found police were "three times *less* likely to shoot unarmed black suspects than unarmed white suspects." "We need to move beyond the post-Ferguson atmosphere where all use of force against a racial/ethnic minority person is considered biased and unreasonable until proven otherwise," they said.

Back in 2001, another study by *The Washington Post* found that police officers were more likely to be killed by black people, rather than vice versa. Specifically, it noted that blacks committed 43 percent of cop killings, despite being just 13 percent of the U.S. population. Data from ProPublica (a center-left organization) found that 62 percent of black people shot by police between 2005 and 2009 were either resisting arrest or assaulting an officer.

David Klinger, a criminology professor at the University of Missouri–St. Louis, studied more than three hundred cops to find that "multiple" officers were disinclined to use deadly force against a black suspect—even when it was permitted.

Conversely, black offenders committed 52 percent of homicides in America between 1980 and 2008. According to the Bureau of Justice Statistics, 93 percent of black victims were killed by other African Americans, while 84 percent of white victims were killed by other Caucasians.

More white children live in poverty than any other race. Data from the National Center for Children in Poverty (NCCP) placed America's 13 million poor kids into the following categories: 4.2 million are Caucasian, 4 million are Latino, 3.6 million are African American, and 400,000 are Asian. Another 200,000 are American Indian. Sure, this might make sense given that the white population is much bigger, but it proves "white privilege" is questionable.

"Poverty affects children of all colors, contrary to stereotypes. The notion held by many Americans that poverty is not a white problem is simply false," said Dr. Jane Knitzer, director of NCCP.

"The sooner all Americans realize these facts about poverty, the better chance we have of eradicating it."

Nearly half of all black men who died in 2015 in age group 15 to 24 died from homicide. In comparison, white men in the same age group died from homicide at a rate of approximately 8 percent. Their most likely cause of death? Unintended injuries from car accidents (according to the Centers for Disease Control and Prevention).

Oh, and the U.S. House of Representatives and Senate have never been more diverse. They currently have 116 lawmakers who are nonwhite, which is more than ever, says the Congressional Research Service.

None of these facts mean that racism doesn't exist. It simply means the issue isn't black and white, like the groupthink might suggest.

THE "WAR" ON WOMEN

Western women are not oppressed. There, I said it.

This doesn't mean they live perfect lives, but then again, neither do men. This is because the world is not a safe space and bad things happen to good people (of both genders).

Despite this, we're constantly told that today's women are an oppressed class, trapped in a state of perpetual bondage (no, not the fun kind).

Historically, this may have been true, but it's not today. In fact, American women have never been more liberated in our country's 244-year history, *which is a good thing*. Feminists: feel free to smile!

Let's look at the data . . .

Women dominate universities in more than one hundred countries, according to the World Economic Forum. And, nope, this isn't a phenomenon exclusive to the West.

Here are a few examples: In Panama, 53 percent *of the entire female population* go into higher education, compared with just 34 percent of men. In Malaysia, nearly 65 percent of university students are female. In Argentina, 98 percent of women have some form of higher education qualification—nearly twice as many as their male counterparts. Similarly, Sri Lankan women outnumber guys in college by almost 2-to-1.

The numbers are similar in America. Data from the National Center for Education Statistics, which is politically neutral, showed that women made up more than 56 percent of college students nationwide in 2018. Across the pond, the United Kingdom's higher-education admissions service, UCAS, notes that women were 36 percent more likely to apply to university than men in 2018—a new record. This is not oppression.

Women are also much less likely to be victims of homicide. A 2013 study by the United Nations Office on Drugs and Crime found that nearly 80 percent of murder victims were male, not female. In fact, women are less likely to be victims of every crime, except rape and sexual assault.

Women also get treated better online. As noted by Pew Research, men are the primary targets of threats (10 percent compared with 6 percent for women). Men are also twice as likely to be harassed for their political views (19 percent of men compared with 10 percent of women).

Similarly, half of all online trolls are women. A study conducted by U.K. think tank Demos analyzed Twitter for three weeks. It found 6,500 different users were targeted by 10,000 "explicitly aggressive and misogynistic" tweets. Fifty percent of them were sent from females who used the terms *slut* and *whore* to describe other women.

Considering these facts about modern-day women, it's just as easy to apply an oppression narrative to men as it is to apply it to women. In fact, recent data supports the idea that men are as oppressed, if not more oppressed, as women are.

More than 93.3 percent of federal inmates are male. This, in part, is because women enjoy the benefits of a criminal sentencing gap. Research conducted by Sonja Starr at the University of Michigan found that men are given much higher sentences (63 percent more) than women convicted of the same crimes in federal court. Women are also significantly more likely to avoid charges and convictions entirely, plus twice as likely to avoid prison if convicted— even if they have the same criminal background.

Meanwhile, American men have been forced to register for Selective Service since 1980. Women are not.

When you look at the facts, women seem clearly better off. They even live longer lives. This is partly because of health initiatives like Obamacare—or the Affordable Care Act (ACA)—which gave them preferential treatment. The ACA had 134 references to "women's health" but only two that were specific to men. Staggering stuff considering the average American man will live to age 76, while the average woman will live to age 81, according to the CDC.

Women win custody of the child in more than 80 percent of all divorces. In 2010, the U.S. Census Bureau reported that nearly fourteen million parents had primary custody of a child after a separation—but only one in six were fathers.

Men also pay more in taxes. OK, this might be because there

are more men in full-time work, but it's still women who take the most from the public purse in state handouts. The data was published in the economics journal *The Review of Income and Wealth*, which referenced a 2015 study called "Income and Fiscal Incidence by Age and Gender." It showed that globally, men cough up the most cash in tax liabilities.

Women also enjoy safer working environments. According to the Bureau of Labor Statistics, 4,492 men died at work in 2015 (92.9 percent of the total) compared with just 344 women (7.1 percent of the total).

All of this data suggests that, in contrast with the mainstream narrative, which is pushed by the likes of Michelle Obama, Jane Fonda, and Bette Midler, women are not an oppressed class. Sure, some of them will experience some discrimination, some of the time, but it's not *systemic*. In fact, women are actively thriving above men and boys in many critical domains.

But if one still needs a reason to justify being a militant feminist, then head over to the Middle East. That's where you'll find real misogyny, which is propped up by a proper patriarchy. Happy travels!

WAGE GAP

There are two things that could survive a nuclear war: cockroaches and the myth of the gender pay gap.

Despite being debunked by countless economists (many of whom are women), it's a statistical lie that never dies. So let's check the facts . . .

First, the claim women earn 79 cents for every man's dollar is pure spin. The figure is an aggregate one, which compares the median of all women's earnings with the equivalent for all men, but this ignores job type, experience, and hours worked. When these factors are considered, the so-called gap disappears faster than conservative content on Twitter.

The Bureau of Labor Statistics shows that men work longer hours. In 2017, men worked an average of 8.4 hours compared to 7.8 hours for women.

In 2009, the U.S. Department of Labor released a paper that examined more than 50 peer-reviewed studies and concluded that the wage gap could almost entirely be explained by the choices made by men and women—including what they studied in college.

In 2018, research conducted by Georgetown University economist Anthony Carnevale showed that women took majors that led to lower-paying jobs (early childhood education, communication disorders sciences and services, and nursing), whereas men chose higher-paying subjects, such as computer science and math.

Women also make different life choices. They're the only gender that can get pregnant (please don't cancel me), so they frequently choose to start families and raise children. Research by the University of Michigan and University of California show that 40 percent of women leave STEM fields—science, technology, engineering, and math—after starting a family. Just 23 percent of men do.

That said, young women who don't have kids are outearning their male peers. According to data from the U.S. Census Bureau's American Community Survey, unmarried, childless females under age 30 who live in cities earn 8 percent more than their male peers in 147 of 150 U.S. cities. In Atlanta and Memphis, the figure is approximately 20 percent more, while young women in New York City, Los Angeles, and San Diego make 17 percent, 12 percent, and 15 percent more, respectively.

Besides, even if men and women do earn different sums, statistical disparity doesn't always mean discrimination—sometimes they are the reward for life choices, which is fair.

This is good news, unless you crave victimhood.

GUN CONTROL

Trigger warning: I'm a supporter of the Second Amendment.

With that out of the way, I also believe there's a sane middle ground between everyone using a bazooka and a blanket ban on firearms.

After all, guns don't shoot people—*people* shoot people. That's why the conversation should be broader, focusing on mental health, the overuse of prescription drugs, and the insidious nature of evil ideologies. But, for now, let's shoot down some misinformation with facts . . .

The number of firearm background checks initiated through the National Instant Criminal Background Check System, or NICS, has almost doubled from 2008 to 2015—yet America's violent crime rate has been in free-fall for decades. The homicide rate fell to 4.8 homicides per 100,000 in 2010, its lowest level in four decades, figures from the Bureau of Justice Statistics show.

The number of guns in America has increased by 50 percent since 1993, while the number of gun-related homicides has fallen by 50 percent in the exact same period. Don't believe me? Ask *New York Times* columnist Nicholas Kristof, who referenced this fact in his article "Some Inconvenient Gun Facts for Liberals," from January 2016.

It's a miracle the mob didn't put him on the firing line for this.

Roughly 89 percent of guns used in crimes "changed hands at least once before recovery by law enforcement," according to the Bureau of Alcohol, Tobacco, and Firearms, and only about 11 percent of these crime guns were purchased legally from federal firearms licensees, or FFLs.

Contrary to popular belief, assault rifles are *not* the preferred choice of weapon for fatal shootings. Most firearm-related killings are carried out with handguns. FBI statistics for 2016 show that handguns caused 7,105 deaths, while rifles caused 374.

Furthermore, four times as many people in the United States are killed with knives or cutting instruments than with all rifles combined. FBI data shows that 1,604 people were killed by the former category in 2016. That number increased the following year, with knives responsible for 1,691 murders in 2017.

Suicide accounts for 60 percent of America's gun-related deaths, reported the *Annual Review of Public Health* in 2015.

A 2013 study ordered by the Centers for Disease Control and Prevention (conducted by the National Academies' Institute of Medicine and National Research Council) reported that up to three million lives were *saved* by defensive gun use in 2008.

A University of Melbourne report concluded the following in 2008: "There is little evidence to suggest that [the Australian mandatory gun-buyback program] had any significant effects on firearm homicides."

In summation, strict gun laws aren't a magic bullet.

HATE CRIMES

Just like supply for "Nazis" frequently fails to meet demand, the same can be said for hate crimes. We're constantly told that these are increasingly common in response to Donald Trump's presidency, but a number of recent hoaxes, including the infamous Jussie Smollett case, show progressives are filling a void with fake claims.

This doesn't mean real hate crimes don't happen, of course, but the evidence paints a complicated picture. And one that undermines the assumption that perpetrators are always straight white men in MAGA hats.

Kentucky State University political science professor Wilfred Reilly (who just so happens to be black, if that sort of thing matters to you) documented four hundred cases of hate-crime hoaxes between 2015 and 2019—and they're just the ones that have been exposed.

"There's very little brutally violent racism in modern [America]," he told *USA Today*. "There are less than 7,000 real hate crimes reported in a typical year. Interracial crime is quite rare; 84 percent of white murder victims and 93 percent of black murder victims are killed by criminals of their own race, and the person most likely to kill you is your ex-wife or ex-husband.

"When violent interracial crimes do occur, whites are at least as likely to be the targets as are minorities," he added. "Simply put, Klansmen armed with nooses are not lurking on Chicago street corners."

Specifically, FBI data for 2017 shows that while 48.6 percent of race-crime victims were black, 17.1 percent were white—three times more than Native Americans, who experienced 5 percent of them.

When it comes to religion, it's not anti-Muslim sentiment that is most common, but anti-Semitism. Of those who suffered religious hate crimes, 58.1 percent of them were Jewish, compared with 18.6 percent who were Muslim.

FBI records from 2017 show that—out of 5,084 attacks on people, rather than on their property—44.9 percent of victims suffered "intimidation," rather than physical violence. This means hate crimes don't even need to include human touch. Often, they're just words, which may hurt feelings but should not be a crime.

By this metric, everyone on Twitter should be locked up for life.

ENVIRONMENTAL ISSUES

Disclaimer: I am not denying that global warming is real or that human beings aren't a contributing factor. I'm no scientist, so I'm inclined to believe what experts tell us.

That said, I'm also a big fan of rational thinking and a sane middle ground. So, when certain members of Congress declare we'll all be dead in twelve years, I prefer to reassure myself with the following . . .

Food Shortage

Back in 1968, Stanford University biologist Paul Ehrlich predicted we'd completely run out of food in short order.

"In the 1970s hundreds of millions of people will starve to death in spite of any crash programs embarked upon now," he wrote in his book *The Population Bomb*. "At this late date nothing can prevent a substantial increase in the world death rate."

Needless to say, he was way off. In fact, I'm eating a delicious

Chipotle burrito right now (with double chicken). According to humanprogress.org, the world's population increased from 4.46 to 7.55 billion between 1980 and 2017, yet resources have become *more* abundant—by 379.6 percent, to be precise.

"The world's resources are finite in the same way that the number of piano keys is finite," wrote think tank policy analyst Marian L. Tupy.

"The instrument has only 88 notes, but those can be played in an infinite variety of ways. The same applies to our planet. The Earth's atoms may be fixed, but the possible combinations of those atoms are infinite. What matters, then, is not the physical limits of our planet, but human freedom to experiment and reimagine the use of resources that we have."

Extreme Weather

The world's death rate from extreme weather is lower than it's been in any decade since 1900, according to the Reason Foundation.

From 1920 to 1929 there were 241 deaths a year per million people, but that figure reduced to 5.4 deaths per million between 2000 and 2010. This includes deaths by everything from hurricanes to floods and "extreme temperatures."

"Overall mortality around the world is increasing, while mortality from weather events is decreasing," said Dr. Indur Goklany, the author behind the study.

"Despite the intense media coverage of storms and climate change's prominent role in political debates, humanity is coping far better with extreme weather events than it is with other much more important health and safety problems."

Polar Bears

If you saw Al Gore's documentary *An Inconvenient Truth*, then you'll be pleased to know that the global polar bear population has actually increased since the 1960s.

(Interestingly, Al never mentions how he sold his failed TV network, Current TV, to Al Jazeera, the state-owned Qatari propaganda channel, for $500 million. Oh, and Qatar is one of the biggest oil exporters in the world. Strange. Wouldn't you say?)

According to Danish environmentalist Bjørn Lomborg, the greatest threat to polar bears comes from hunters, who shoot between three hundred and five hundred of them every year—not global warming.

If this doesn't suggest to you that the environmental thing is part BS, then here's another reality check.

The panic is best summarized by British journalist and author Matt Ridley, who told me: "Global warming is real, but slower than expected. The latest hysteria is based on exaggeration rather than evidence.

"We are told that we must panic, despair, and deliberately impose harsh austerity on ordinary people just in case the current gentle warming of the climate turns nasty at some point later in the century.

"That is like taking chemotherapy for a head cold."

If you're interested in a sane solution to climate change (driven by reason and not panic) that doesn't involve a giant takeover of multiple industries, see the work being done by the American Conservative Coalition, founded by former *Rubin Report* guest Benji Backer. Free markets might just have some of the answers to our climate problems, and we shouldn't be afraid to explore them.

REPUBLICANS = BAD, DEMOCRATS = GOOD

I can't believe this needs stating, but here goes: Democrats aren't necessarily "good" and Republicans aren't inherently "bad." Human beings are a complex mix of both, just like the political parties they represent.

So it always makes me raise an eyebrow when Democrats claim to occupy the moral high ground. Especially when you consider their history, which lurches from defending slavery to founding the Ku Klux Klan.

In fact, here are some little-known facts from PragerU about the party of love and tolerance:

- Back in 1854, many Democrats supported slavery and wanted it to expand. When a number of outraged members disagreed, they broke away and, alongside members of the Whig Party, formed the Republican Party—which actively *opposed* slavery.
- In 1856, the first Republican presidential candidate, John C. Frémont, ran against a Democrat on just nine manifesto points . . . six of which related to equality for black people.
- The following year, the U.S. Supreme Court approved the Dred Scott ruling, which declared that black Americans were "not persons but property." Which party ran the Supreme Court? The Democrats.
- They surpassed themselves in the 1860s, when the Ku Klux Klan was formed by Democrat Nathan Bedford

Forrest. A year later Democrats also created the Confederate flag.

- Soon after, in 1865, Republican President Abraham Lincoln, who was trying to abolish slavery, was shot and killed by John Wilkes Booth (yup, a Democrat).
- The Democratic Party then opposed a hat trick of legislative changes that would've liberated black people: the Thirteenth Amendment (abolishment of slavery), the Fourteenth Amendment (citizenship), and the Fifteenth Amendment (which gave black people the vote). They all later passed thanks to Republican support.
- Several decades later, in 1912, Democrat Woodrow Wilson was elected president. The following year he showed the first film to be screened in the White House—*The Birth of a Nation*, which was essentially KKK propaganda.
- By 1918 Wilson had banned any criticism of the government via the controversial Espionage and Sedition Acts.
- Jump forward to 1964 and the biggest congressional opposition to the Civil Rights Act came from Democrats.
- The following year, President Lyndon B. Johnson, a Democrat, launched his War on Poverty, which was billed as correcting racially related poverty. At this time, the out-of-wedlock birth rate was 25 percent among blacks (according to the Office of Policy Planning and Research). In 2015 it was 77 percent. Dr. Thomas Sowell described this phenomenon by saying, "The black family, which had survived centuries of slavery and discrimination, began rapidly disintegrating in the

liberal welfare state that subsidized unwed pregnancy and changed welfare from an emergency rescue to a way of life."

- Today, Democrats oppose school choice, a decision that can trap (mostly black) children in failing schools, while politically correct policing often leaves black neighborhoods at the mercy of violent crime.
- And let's not forget, candidates Hillary Clinton and Barack Obama both opposed gay marriage during their first runs for the White House. It's not too hard to imagine the progressives of 2040 demanding that the Obama Presidential Library be taken down due to his obvious homophobia, is it?

Of course, none of this history dictates the Democrats' future, just as none of your history dictates yours, but it should remind you that no political party defines "goodness."

This knowledge is power and you should be empowered, especially when it comes to politicians who will say anything to get your vote.

None of the above are my opinions. They're cold, hard facts. I'm merely presenting them here for your consideration.

Of course, standing up for yourself with facts will almost certainly lead you to the next battle, which involves an angry horde.

6

Never Surrender to the Mob

I T'S NOVEMBER 2014, and I'm about to commit professional suicide.

The Rubin Report has been picked up by Larry King's Ora TV, which is his first big media venture since leaving CNN.

The greatest interviewer of all time has chosen me to be part of his new digital network, which has already earned itself an Emmy nomination for its content.

Each week, I'm sitting down with critical thinkers, authors, and philosophers to discuss important issues that the mainstream media ignores—and the result is catching fire with people all over the world. It's everything I've been working toward for the past two decades, and after countless years of lesser gigs, such as bartending, waiting tables, and retail, I've finally made it.

Except, there's a problem . . . a huge problem. I need to tell the talk show legend that I'm pulling the plug on the show just two months after we signed the deal. Then, once I drop that bomb, I need to do the same with my director, my producer, and the rest of the staff before posting one final video to shut everything down.

This isn't going to be easy. In fact, it's going to be near impossible.

I love my work. I *live* my work. There's nothing else I'd rather be doing with my life—well, except play in the NBA—but at this point I'm nearly forty years old, I've got a bad right ankle, and I'm only five foot eleven.

Unfortunately, the decision to quit isn't exclusively mine. My hand is being forced by the universe, which has given me a secret that's becoming increasingly difficult to hide: I'm sick. So sick, in fact, that my hair is falling out at a shocking rate.

Each day I wake up to find clumps of it strewn across my pillow, replaced by three-inch bald patches at the back of my head.

Initially, it starts as one or two random spots, which I can dismiss, but they soon grow in size and number, spreading like wildfire. Within weeks I've lost nearly a third of my hair and it's becoming harder to disguise with sprays and sprinkle-on fibers, which can only do so much . . . especially when I'm positioned in front of hot studio lights and high-definition cameras.

The mere act of trying to conceal it becomes a feedback loop from hell: the more I worry, the worse it gets. Soon, stray hairs start falling onto my shoulders mid-broadcast, causing me to bristle every time a camera zooms in or a crew member gets too close.

Making matters worse, I'm acutely aware this paper-thin facade can't last forever—the shedding is fast encroaching my front hairline, which I've already decided is game over. If that goes, I go. Not just because of vanity, but because I don't want the show to become a pity party. I want it to be about big ideas and diverse thought, not a reality TV series starring yours truly.

Besides, even if I wanted to, how would I begin to articulate what was happening to me?

At this stage I'm still searching for a diagnosis. Is it cancer? Or AIDS? Can it be treated—or is it chronic? Am I dying? Whatever the answer, it's got me shedding like a Siberian husky in the dead of summer.

After days of searching the symptoms online (something you should never do when you're sick), I eventually found a doctor in Santa Monica, who specializes in trichology: the science of hair and scalp. Typically, I love driving everywhere, because it's a welcome break from all the online madness. But this time it's different. I'm way too anxious to be behind the wheel, so my husband, David, takes the reins as I wilt into the passenger seat.

Fast-forward an hour and we're finally at the clinic, where the doctor—who's only recently taken over the practice and is way too young to inspire confidence in us—bluntly breaks the news that I have alopecia areata, an autoimmune disease that attacks the hair follicles.

This, she tells me, is typically caused by sudden or intense stress and, unfortunately, there's no magic bullet when it comes to treatment. Some people do nothing and make complete recoveries, while others try everything and still lose their hair.

Worse still, she can tell by the existing patterns on my scalp that it's moving toward my face and may soon spread to the rest of my body, including my genitals. *Great*, I think. *Just what I've always wanted: bald balls.*

And with that, I see everything good slipping away from me: my job, my income, my self-esteem, and in a worst-case scenario, my marriage. After all, who would want to be with somebody who's a shadow of his former self?

My best bet, the doctor insists, is to identify the root cause of my stress (no pun intended) and manage it accordingly. Otherwise, I risk being completely hairless, possibly forever, even losing my eyebrows and eyelashes.

To do this, I see just one realistic solution on the horizon: walking away from the minefield that is political discourse, which has become more brutal than I ever anticipated.

While my show has tapped into something relevant with smart, open-minded people all across the globe, I've also experienced an equal and opposite reaction—namely, the hate I'm getting from the left has turned from a trickle into a biblical flood. And it's clearly getting to me.

I'm not just talking about angry tweets from trolls who I could block or mute with the touch of a button, although I get plenty of that. I'm referring to real vitriol from people who know me. Friends and former colleagues. These attacks cut much deeper.

Suddenly, longtime friends are leaving venomous voice mails, calling me racist and misogynistic, while others send emails denouncing me as a hateful bigot who deserves to die. All of these insane, over-the-top insults are shocking to me, but one memorable tirade hits me like a punch in the gut.

One Sunday afternoon—a couple of weeks before my symptoms suddenly appear—my phone blew up with a string of expletive-laden text messages from a friend and former costar of *The Young Turks*.

This person, who I won't name, was like a sister to me during my time at the network. She'd even been invited to my wedding a few months earlier.

Yet, despite our long and loyal history, something was amiss.

Although she publicly prided herself—no, *bragged*—about being a tolerant liberal, she wouldn't respect my new views because they didn't match hers. According to the religion of progressives, of which she was a devout follower, I was an apostate and should be treated as such.

"Your shit-talking is outta control!" she ranted in the first of her messages. "The social justice warriors you whine about fought for *your* rights [as a gay man]. But fuck 'em, right? If they don't hate Muslims they're worthless to you."

Stunned by this total spin on reality, I reread the words several times to try to find the punch line, but there wasn't one. "Good Lord, you must be kidding," I reply. "I don't hate anyone on their religion, skin color, or anything else."

"You're an opportunist," she hits back. "You don't give a flying fuck about friendship. Your bigotry is very clear. It's what your entire career is about now."

"Yes, you got me!" I joke, trying to diffuse the situation with humor. "I was secretly a bigot all these years. We can agree to disagree and leave it there."

But it keeps on coming.

"I've seen it all, Dave, I don't need any more disappointment [from you]. You're a fucking opportunistic pig. Fuck you! You're fucking insane and completely lack self-awareness . . . you literally have no shame, it's incredible. Good luck with your 'show'!"

Eventually, the messages stop and I'm slack-jawed by the irony of it all. In her eyes she's the tolerant liberal and I'm the new Anita Bryant (ask your mother if you're under forty).

This was the very first time I'd personally experienced the left's absolute hatred for dissent—and it truly hurt. Their level of disgust resonated with me for days and, to some extent, it felt like a weird form of PTSD.

Foolishly, rather than talk about it, I decided to internalize everything—which ultimately caused it to manifest physically. Now, I'm suddenly sitting in a doctor's office and dealing with the literal fallout . . . from my head.

Fortunately, I get a glimmer of hope when it's suggested that I try an alternative and fairly experimental treatment called diphency-prone, or DPCP. This involves applying a powerful formula directly to my scalp, twice a day, which deliberately sparks an allergic reaction. The theory is that my white blood cells then attack this response, rather than waging a war on my hair follicles.

Desperate and genuinely scared, I give it a chance and feel a fleeting sense of optimism. But it doesn't last long. From the very first application of the treatment, my body totally freaks out. It's hard to believe, but the side effects turn out to be much, much worse than the actual hair loss.

First, I develop itchy, relentless rashes all over my body, which make me scratch constantly—even while on camera. Then, I become sensitive to temperature, meaning I struggle to cope with even low-level heat, which is hardly ideal when living in Southern California. Then my moods begin to fluctuate, my concentration fades, I look exhausted and become visibly bloated, and except for doing *The Rubin Report,* I never want to go out.

Looking back at videos of myself from this time—the exact moment my career was supposed to be taking off—is pretty painful. My "Why I Left the Left" video for PragerU was recorded smack-dab in the middle of it all. See for yourself; the person in it is drowning, not waving.

Slowly, I retreat into myself and it becomes an isolated time. It's tough to describe exactly how I felt during this period, but it was a pretty dark chapter. Sleepless nights ensued, I lost my appetite, and I actively avoided everyone. Before this, David and I had hosted friends for dinner at least once a week and went out another night or two as well. Now, I don't want anyone coming over, nor do I want to visit others.

Besides David, the only other person who knows about this is my hairstylist, Jess, who first spotted the problem a couple of months earlier. But both are sworn to secrecy and I'm desperate to keep this all under wraps.

But even in the privacy of my own home, I can't escape it. Every part of my existence is affected, including my sex life. I don't want to be seen naked, much less touched. I've got disgusting, gooey sores on my scalp, which ooze blood and mucus down my neck. Trust me, this does not put you in the mood for love!

But I persist. Encouraged by the doctor—who doesn't take insurance, meaning the $10,000 costs are coming out of my pocket—I try to keep the faith and finish the full course of treatment, which spans nine months.

Unfortunately, I don't get anywhere near that far down the line. The nightmare reaches its nadir one evening in West Hollywood when I'm only halfway through it.

Bent on lifting my spirits, David drags me out for dinner with our director, Amiria, to a trendy new restaurant on Melrose Avenue called E.P.&L.P. One of the hottest places in L.A., it's a destination point for the cool crowd. Everyone there is either a celebrity or a model (of which I look and feel like neither).

Suddenly, while unwittingly standing under a heat lamp on the rooftop bar, I'm overcome with a feeling of complete nausea. The color drains from my face and I feel like my scalp is on fire.

The burning sensation cuts across my head, then shoots down into my shoulders, arms, and hands. My whole body feels like it's on fire, I'm dripping with sweat, and my shirt begins sticking to me.

I've got to get out of here, I think as I scan the room to identify an escape route through the hordes of people. By this point sweat is pouring down my face and I feel like I'm about to collapse. Am I having a heart attack?

Panicked, I push my way through the crowd and leave. Alone, I burst out into the street and catch my breath before staggering the few blocks home. Once inside, I head straight to the bathroom and puke in the toilet.

Splattered in vomit, I take a cold shower—hairs still falling out around me, gross gunk running down my face, and—for the first time since my grandmother's death five years earlier—I burst into tears. I'm physically and emotionally drained. I'm done.

I've got no more fight left in me and reluctantly concede defeat.

I crawl into bed and think how to tell my family, my audience, and my mentor that I'm ending *The Rubin Report,* just as it's getting good. Whatever healthy discourse I'd managed to bring back into the political arena is coming with a stress that's ravaging my personal health.

The next morning, I wake up with my head stuck to the pillow . . . like I had done for the previous six months. I roll over and grab my phone to call Larry King, who I decide should be the first to know. Then something happens to me as I lay there, waiting for the call to connect.

I realize that I'd hit rock bottom—and survived. It wasn't a particularly dramatic moment. There were no lightning bolts or thunderclaps. No visual hallucinations to speak of. It was just a quiet realization of the fact that I was down, but not out.

In that moment everything changed.

Fuck this, I think to myself. Giving up on everything now would be ridiculous. Like Luke Skywalker rejecting the lightsaber from Obi-Wan. Or Neo choosing the blue pill.

So I gave myself a good old-fashioned reality check.

Both of my grandfathers were in the U.S. Air Force during World War II, which killed tens of millions, in dire circumstances. My maternal grandfather, David—who I'm named after—was a bombardier and fought on the front line.

Meanwhile, my paternal grandfather, Aaron, was a military mechanic. They experienced real conflict—not just the culture war we're seeing now. And they had much greater hardships than I.

How could I not be a little bit brave after everything they went through? What would they think if they saw me living in a time of unprecedented freedom, yet was too afraid to exercise my own damn voice?

OK, I'd lost some friends and a whole bunch of hair, which wasn't ideal, but they were both a necessary consequence of being myself. They're now battle scars to be proud of, which is why I'm telling you this story. It has a happy ending.

Ultimately, I survived and so did *The Rubin Report*. My hair has now (mostly) grown back, and with it has come a new philosophical approach to all the drama. Namely, that shit happens— but caving in to the haters doesn't fix it.

Fast-forward to today—literally right now as I type this—and my phone is blowing up once again. This time it's not abuse from a former friend, but messages from Fox News' Tucker Carlson.

It's March 2019 and the TV anchor is experiencing his own

leftist lynching after decade-old comments of his were dug up and used to try to destroy him.

The people behind it are members of Media Matters for America, a far-left nonprofit that uses its connections to tattletale on anyone who dares to question the social justice warrior agenda. I'm not going to bother detailing what his comments were because they're beyond irrelevant. Media Matters is only digging into Carlson's past because it fears his influence in the present.

The organization's bigger agenda, however, is to silence the average person—including you.

Just a day earlier, I was on Tucker's show to discuss this very matter.

"Did we overestimate the willingness of the Democratic establishment to coexist with people who disagree with them?" Tucker asks. "And did we underestimate the real, existential threat to free speech that we now have?"

"I wish I could say that this whole situation is shocking," I reply. "But it's exactly what I've been raising the alarm about on my show for the past five years. Not apologizing is exactly the right thing to do. That's exactly the message your audience—and the average American—needs to hear.

"We've watched years of the mob coming for everybody. It's time we stop giving in to it. Not just so that a guy like you isn't taken out, but the average American doesn't fear that something they said twenty years ago might be used against them today.

"That idea of mutually assured destruction is not the America that I want to be part of. I want to be part of something that has a little bit of forgiveness, that understands we're all imperfect creatures and is a little more respectful of our ability to disagree, which our country was founded on."

"So how can people fight back and stand strong?" he asks me, pulling his trademark "puzzled" face. To answer, I dig deep into my own experience and tell it straight.

"Start speaking up, now!" I say. "This [question] comes up at every public event I do. This is what young people are asking about: 'I'm afraid to speak up . . . I wanna get the grade or I don't wanna get fired from my job.'

"Imagine if everyone started saying something. If more of us start doing it. They can't take us all down. And if we don't say something, then we'll get what we deserve, which is something far, far worse than what we've got now."

As the segment closes, I take a brief moment to reflect.

Somehow, in the three and a half years since almost ending *The Rubin Report*, I'd not only survived leaving the left, but thrived. If somebody had told me this a few years earlier, I wouldn't have believed them, but it's true.

This means it can be true for you too—as long as you never, ever surrender to the mob.

Because I'd rather you not lose half the hair on your head and go on an awful experimental treatment to regain it, allow me to offer you some tips for surviving when you're in the eye of the storm:

- **Stand tough.** You can only become the kind of person you admire through surviving hardship. As human beings, we usually only learn to take life seriously when our world comes into question. So although a mob attack might seem like a worst-case scenario, recognize that it's actually an opportunity for growth and self-discovery. Then act upon it.

- **Never apologize.** This means having the courage of your convictions, right when the pile-on is at its most intense. At this point, it might be tempting to wave the white flag of surrender and apologize, but don't do it. This is the precise moment when you must keep going with your head held high.

- **Accept that you'll lose friends.** Everything clicks once you start figuring out who you are, but the process of self-discovery is often painful, requiring you to let go of people. Fight hard to maintain your friendships, especially the old ones, but don't be anyone's doormat. At some point you may have to let someone go. This is very sad, but embrace it like you would any breakup. And believe it or not, you'll make new friends who'll accept you exactly for who you are.

None of this is a guarantee that "it gets better." Life won't suddenly be wonderful. Bad stuff will still happen. But at the end of the day, you will own your life, it'll be on you, and you'll have integrity.

As the old saying goes, if you have integrity, nothing else matters. But if you don't have integrity, nothing else matters.

Now if you're still unclear about any of this, go to YouTube and play Frank Sinatra's "My Way." Trust me, you'll get it by the end of the song.

Now that you have the chutzpah to resist the mob, you'll be better off if you can learn to anticipate them before they ambush you. In the next chapter, you'll learn how to shrug off all of the lazy arguments about race, patriotism, and gender that'll be thrown your way.

7

Stop Hating (Straight) White Men, America, and Western Values

ALLOW ME TO open this chapter with a statement that's wildly controversial and gulagworthy hate speech: America is the greatest country in the history of the world.

If you're triggered by this, stop reading. Take a few moments to collect yourself—go outside for some fresh air, do a little light stretching, or center your thoughts through mindful meditation.

Whatever you do, only return to these highly flammable pages once you're ready to confront the truth that America is the best country on Earth (and Earth is the best planet in the galaxy!).

If you disagree with this, then you should probably ditch all of your first-world luxuries—including but not limited to your iPhone, PlayStation, seventy-inch flat-screen TV, and Netflix subscription, plus your right to live freely in a representative democracy—and go elsewhere. Ideally, a place where you can feel morally superior while living in squalor or under an oppressive regime.

A socialist dystopia like Venezuela would be an excellent choice, or perhaps a dictatorship such as North Korea. Sure, you'll have to eat out of the garbage or surrender your passport, but hey, just think of all the points you'll get with the "woke" crew. The retweets alone will make it all worthwhile!

Of course, these people will still be living stateside, because most morally confused leftists never leave the comfort of the United States. In fact, they're total hypocrites when it comes to opposing American exceptionalism (or whatever you want to call the belief that living here is the ultimate privilege).

Instead of simply expressing gratitude for the "land of opportunity" and everything it offers, they prefer to feel guilty about it—or at least pretend to feel guilty about it, which is the crucial difference.

See, it's all subterfuge to deflect attention from their gilded lives.

Woke celebrities such as Lena Dunham, Amy Schumer, and Kathy Griffin are prime examples. They all promised to emigrate if Trump won the 2016 election, but they're still here, reaping the benefits of living in an affluent, opportunity-rich country where they're safe and free. Which is precisely why they never leave.

I'm not just dissing women here either. Plenty of male actors are just as bad—Chris Evans, Mark Ruffalo, and Mark Hamill endlessly rail against the "oppressive" U.S. regime while plundering every benefit from it. Yes, that's right. Captain America, The Hulk, and Luke Skywalker are all members of the hypocritical superelite.

Ironically, those who do flee America are usually rich people wanting to escape being taxed to the hilt by greedy politicians and the IRS. Something that's only going to get worse when future president Bernie Sanders or Elizabeth Warren executes Order 66 to eliminate the remaining billionaires scattered across the galaxy.

And that's the suspicious thing about the left's self-loathing.

The worst offenders tend to be the most successful—the ones who've benefited most from Western values and institutions such as capitalism and pluralism. They've climbed to the top and are now pulling the ladder up behind them.

Except it's not just celebrities who virtue signal their misguided shame. It's huge swathes of the population, from school kids to office colleagues and family relatives.

I'm not saying these people are inherently bad, of course, but their motivation certainly isn't noble: they're just greasing the wheels of the system for their own selfish benefit (though many of them don't even know it; basically they're useful idiots).

This is because outward virtue signaling is separate from being a considerate, moral person. Whereas the latter is central for common decency (and is something we should all strive for), the former is just a display of faux morality. One that's designed to offer protection from the mob ever turning on them. It's a protection racket—a form of insurance. You scratch my back, I'll scratch yours.

See, developing your own views—and speaking them, even if your voice shakes—takes tenacity. It requires conscience. It's about choosing the path of *most* resistance, not opting for the easier route with fewer hurdles . . . even though I understand why people frequently make that choice. It requires no thinking—resorting to your factory settings and repeating the left's insipid mantras about the world. It's like putting your out-of-office alert on every day. Except you haven't checked out for a well-deserved vacation (more on that later—we all need to decompress). You've simply dodged unpleasant realities through denial.

In psychologyspeak, this is called avoidance behavior—a maladaptive quality that gives us the illusion of short-term relief, but can actually make things worse in the long run.

So, in this chapter, I'm going to counter this by telling you to check your privilege—and be thankful for it. See, you are privileged—we all live in a Western society, and that's a truly amazing thing. It's the result of hard work by our ancestors over many centuries.

Furthermore, it's important to know just how good we have it, so that we can recognize true injustice when we see it—especially government corruption and authoritarianism—then destroy it.

This is particularly important, because many authoritarian dystopias *do* exist in today's world, and current left-wing thinking risks importing their flawed principles, such as communism and socialism, into our country.

This would be a huge mistake, because without American ideals such as free speech, freedom of religion, and free markets, we'd risk the sort of violence and oppression that's been playing out on the streets of Hong Kong. As I write this, thousands of people have spent months protesting for their freedoms against China's encroaching communist party.

The unrest first began in June 2019 when Hong Kong's leader, Carrie Lam—yes, a woman!—tried to implement a controversial extradition bill, which would've deported people to stand trial in mainland China and Taiwan, where the legal systems are shrouded in secrecy and rooted in socialism (as opposed to Hong Kong's common-law setup, which is based on precedents established by the courts—much like in America).

Proving how envied the U.S. model is, Hong Kong protesters

even sang the "Star Spangled Banner" and begged Donald Trump to intervene in their plight. I know, right—it's the sort of stuff that would leave Debra Messing, Alyssa Milano, and Michael Moore literally shaking! The world not only doesn't hate us, it envies us.

While it's important to remember that living in America is a great privilege, I also don't want you to fixate on it. So, once you've checked your privilege, I want you to move on with your life and stop obsessing over it. Why? Because ditching the victimhood narrative and making your life about more than just politics is a core tenet of classical liberalism. It's all about taking responsibility for your life instead of expecting somebody else, or something else— such as the government—to intervene.

All our heroes, real or fictitious, chose to embrace that responsibility.

Just imagine if Frodo from *Lord of the Rings* spent all his time demanding help from the nanny state, rather than completing his mission in the fires of Mount Doom. Or if Atreyu from the movie *The NeverEnding Story* wanted somebody else to hop on Falcor and save Fantasia. Or if literally any main character from any Disney movie in the last fifty years said, "Oh, can't somebody else do it?"

Would we root for them? No, we'd think they were spoiled brats who needed to toughen up and own their lot in life. It may not always be easy for them, but expecting to be rescued is not independence. *And independence is pivotal to being a classical liberal.*

So stop fixating on how many victim points you have (or don't have)—it's a zero-sum game. Instead, just do your thing in this wonderful country of ours.

After all, at this rate, we might not have it for very long . . .

DON'T TAKE YOUR RIGHTS
FOR GRANTED

In case you hadn't noticed, the left wants you to believe that the United States is a lethal cocktail of imperialism, xenophobia, toxic masculinity, and capitalist greed designed to enslave the masses.

This is a fascinating take, considering the left also wants open borders so that everyone can apparently share in the nightmare that is America.

It's a plot so twisted that Wes Craven could've written, directed, and produced it.

First of all, no, we're not an imperialist country. The United States of America was literally founded on a pushback against imperialism, which is defined as "a policy of extending a country's power and influence through colonization, use of military force, or other means."

Remember the "no taxation without representation" Boston Tea Party? Our founders were fighting to be free in their own nation. They were stopping England's King George III from extending his power across the Atlantic Ocean. That's what the American Revolution was all about—thirteen British colonies in North America escaping Europe's imperial rule. We wanted to govern ourselves, and ever since that war ended in 1783, we've stayed true to our belief that nations should self-govern.

That doesn't mean we've always been perfect. There's no doubt that we've made some big mistakes as administrations have changed. For example, most of us now view George W. Bush's invasion of Iraq in 2003 as a massive blunder, escalating into a war that cost thousands of Iraqi lives and millions of American dollars (though it should be noted that until Barack Obama withdrew U.S. troops, free elections were being had and there was hope for a democratic future. Sadly, that's all but lost now, and the debate remains as to whether we should've stayed to help with that transition).

This aside, much of our foreign military intervention has been good—just look at Korea, Vietnam, and both World Wars, where our contribution secured much-needed freedoms.

None of these infamous battle sites are now satellite American states that we've colonized. Hint: they would be if we were imperialists.

Anyone who thinks otherwise probably hasn't (A) learned history or (B) experienced the sort of conflict that requires intervention in the first place.

One person who definitely has is former *Rubin Report* guest Brigitte Gabriel, who grew up in war-torn Lebanon, where she was terrorized by Islamic militants for her Christian faith.

During the country's civil war, which raged from 1975 to 1990 and killed roughly 120,000 people, her home was destroyed in a brutal bomb strike. This forced her family to live in a shelter without running water, heating, or proper sanitation for several years, and to this day, Gabriel still has tiny pieces of shrapnel in her body.

Eventually, she was rescued by some members of the Israel Defense Forces before emigrating to America. Thankfully, she now suffers no religious persecution whatsoever—although she does get hate from progressives, who call her a "white supremacist" (even though she's brown-skinned), and the Southern Poverty Law Center, which refers to her as a "hate group leader."

From her perspective, America isn't a swaggering superpower

trying to dominate the world. It's her savior. One that tries to show other countries the way forward: morally, legally, and economically.

"America is God's gift to the universe!" she tells me. "There is no better place. I came to the United States in 1989 and have never, ever felt like a second-class citizen here. I am so fortunate to live in this country. America is known around the world as the land of dreams and opportunity for a reason.

"Back in 1987, I remember watching a Hollywood movie in Lebanon and asking my American fiancé, 'Is it really possible to live like this in the USA?'

"Today, I not only live better than the characters in that movie, but I have been able to do it on my own as a self-made woman. An opportunity that would have been impossible for me in Lebanon."

In terms of her success, she founded Act for America—the nation's largest national security grassroots organization, which has more than one million members. In addition to this, she's also dined with the U.S. president, although she refuses to tell me how many scoops of ice cream he eats.

Interestingly, human rights activist Ayaan Hirsi Ali has a similar story.

Born in Somalia, where she was the victim of female-genital mutilation at the hands of her grandmother, she personally witnessed the hell of government force when her father was jailed for opposing the country's president, Siad Barre.

When her father managed to escape from prison, the family fled to Kenya in order to start a new life. Years later, in 1992, Ayaan went on the run again—this time to avoid an arranged marriage. She sought refuge in the Netherlands, where she was given temporary asylum.

There, she became a prominent political figure and even took part in a 2004 film called *Submission*, directed by Theo van Gogh (Vincent's distant relative), which criticized the treatment of women in Islam.

Upon its release, van Gogh was murdered in the street by Mohammed Bouyeri, a Dutch-Moroccan Muslim who found the film to be offensive. He shot and stabbed van Gogh in broad daylight, pinning a death threat addressed to Ayaan onto his body.

Terrified, Ayaan escaped to America. Why? Because, unlike everywhere else, she knew it would truly set her free.

Sure enough, she was granted citizenship and the opportunity to pursue happiness, which is the exact same privilege offered to all legal immigrants in America. Now, she's a *New York Times* bestselling author and a scholar at Stanford University's Hoover Institute. She's also a mother of one who's happily married to (shock, horror!) a straight white man of her own choosing, historian Niall Ferguson.

Also a fellow at Stanford, he too explains that, as a military force, the main purpose of America is not to terrorize and impose, but "to spread free markets, to entrench the rule of law so as to eliminate the mainsprings of terrorism, to impose order, and pave the way for representative government."

Today, thanks in part to the freedoms of America, Ayaan has rediscovered the strength to be a vocal critic of radical Islam. Unfortunately, her reward for doing this is to be labeled an extremist by the members of the Southern Poverty Law Center (yes, them again) and to be thrown under the bus by some of America's most prominent progressives, including Jon Stewart.

During an appearance on *The Daily Show*, when she was discussing Islam's oppression of women, he abruptly closed the interview by dismissing all of her valid points by saying, "You'd just like people to buy your book."

For her, it's profoundly absurd that people—specifically, fellow Americans . . . many of them educated, middle-class millennials who've never experienced anything like real hardship—can hate a country that frequently does so much good, both domestically and internationally. Especially for persecuted people living in less fortunate places.

"I love America because it is based on classical liberal principles. Political freedom and free enterprise is what makes America a superpower," she tells me.

"Many recent immigrants like me flourish in America because we are drawn to these principles and, once here, we take the opportunities we find with gratitude and humility."

It's a shame that so much of America's left doesn't share the same thankfulness.

When's the last time a Democrat stood proudly onstage and said words like *freedom, liberty,* or *Constitution*? Surely it's time to show them the light.

LOOK BACKWARD, NOT FORWARD

Naturally, Ayaan's immigration story is hers alone, but it also echoes many of those experienced by our parents and grandparents.

Sadly, the left would have you think that there's no value to our nation's past because it's characterized by white, male oppressors. This mind-set is not only false but also destructive and dangerous.

See, while it's important to think in terms of progress—and

specifically progress toward freedom—we also need to preserve the values of previous generations who make this possible. Doing so fosters an attitude of gratitude, rather than victimhood, and gives us something to strive for.

I, for instance, wouldn't enjoy the freedom and opportunity I do today without the perseverance and struggle of the people who came before me. My family risked everything to come to the United States as immigrants, and I'm sure your elders have a similar story.

My maternal great-grandfather, Joe Jawitz, moved to America from Lithuania in 1916. He traveled by boat with hundreds of others and arrived at Ellis Island with absolutely nothing but determination and the clothes on his back.

After taking several blue-collar jobs to survive, he eventually became a broker at a food company in Brooklyn, which enabled him to get a tiny one-bedroom apartment. During this time he met his wife, my maternal great-grandmother, U.S.-born Bertha Greenhouse. That's right, people—the American girl married an immigrant from Europe!

Eventually, his blood, sweat, and tears paid off and built a decent middle-class existence for them, which in turn helped create the life I enjoy three generations later.

My father's side is no different. My paternal great-grandparents, Isaac and Jennie, moved to America from Belarus in the 1890s. They had five children, all born in the United States—the youngest being my grandpa, Artie.

Like most immigrants from that time, they were so poor that the entire family had to share a studio walk-up on the Lower East Side of Manhattan, where the children crammed into a small double bed.

Tragically, Great-Grandpa Isaac died unexpectedly of appendicitis when he was just thirty-two years old—leaving nine-month-old Artie fatherless. The family was devastated and forced to move to cheaper accommodations because they couldn't afford the rent.

Then, a few years later, Jennie married a man called Hyman Block, who'd also been widowed at a young age. Together they raised her five children, plus his three, in a tiny apartment where resources were tight, but love was free-flowing. Think *The Brady Bunch* but with a much smaller house, way less money, and no laugh track.

My ancestors experienced a real, grinding poverty, but eventually my Grandpa Artie went on to become a lithographer and, during his training, got his first job, which paid him 25 cents per hour (a rate he thought was fantastic). Years later, he married my paternal grandmother, Miriam, and they had three children, including my dad, Ira.

When it was my father's turn to carry the baton, he too worked hard to build on his parents' legacy. This involved commuting to New York City from Long Island five days a week, twice a day, for over thirty years. That's roughly fifteen thousand hours (or two years) of his life spent on the train.

Why did he do it? So that he too could provide a better life for us. Just as his father and grandfather did for their families.

The reward for my father's hard work is that my brother, sister, and I could all attend college and create decent lives for ourselves. My brother is a successful salesman in the media industry and has re-created that suburban dream for his wife and three kids in Westchester, New York, while my sister is a graphic designer with two kids and a husband (a brown-skinned immigrant from Israel!) in Manhattan.

Today, the tale continues with me as I plan to start my own family with David. As I've already mentioned, we're currently in the process of having children through a surrogate—something that's priceless, but likely to cost about $250,000. (I keep telling David we should try the natural way, but it just ain't working.)

Now ask yourself: Would I be bringing a child into this world if America was a menacing matrix of oppression? If I didn't believe our son or daughter could have a wonderful life of their own making? Something that could be as good if not better than mine? No, of course not.

More important, if America was so hateful and homophobic, would it even allow me to have a child in the first place? Gimme a break. In other parts of the world I'd be thrown off a building.

We're at this incredible point in America's evolution because of the people who preceded us. Their struggle is now our privilege. And their legacy is now our freedom.

By this I mean that the idea of "privilege" exists on a continuum— and we're all just at different points on the journey. It's a constant work in progress, and yes, some people are farther along on it than others, but this doesn't mean they haven't earned their place. Or that they can't go backward.

If you live in America today, your family's story is similar, though you might just have to change the dates, the food, and the accents. Don't run from that history. Be proud of it.

To feel guilty that your ancestors worked long and hard to get you ahead is not only disrespectful to them but also an erasure of history—of everything they did to help you survive in the world.

Behavioral psychologist and former *Rubin Report* guest Gad Saad—who fled war-torn Lebanon for America after his parents were kidnapped by Palestinian terrorists—nailed it when he said the left is now characterized by a weird form of self-flagellation.

"The motto is no longer 'I think therefore I am.' It's not even 'I'm a victim therefore I am.' It's now, 'I self-flagellate therefore I am,'" he says. "It's almost a theater of the absurd. The currency is victimhood by proxy. Whoever can grovel the most is the currency of the radical left."

Don't be like them. Be better.

EVERY COUNTRY HAS ITS BAGGAGE

Of course, none of this means we should consider the United States to be without fault—we've already established that it's not. But, hey, every country has its baggage.

Seriously, if Hollywood's woke elite did decide to emigrate, where would they go—Canada? No, because it's freezing and no true American likes hockey.

China? Not so fast. It's a communist dictatorship with a social media credit system. It'll also tell you how many kids you can have and block thousands of websites, including Facebook, Instagram, and Twitter, to maximize mind control.

Not exactly what you'd call liberal, right?

According to Amnesty International, China has also sent more than one million Muslim Uighurs to "re-education camps"—complete with watchtowers and barbed-wire fences—while committing more executions than any other nation. (Don't tell the United Nations about this, because it's more focused on whether a Jew can visit Bethlehem; you know, that place where Jesus was from.)

If you think the current U.S. administration is problematic, listen to this: China's president Xi Jinping could be allowed to rule for life, regardless of what voters do at the ballot box, after essentially rigging the election system.

I suppose there's always Thailand, but our outspoken stars would have to stop their Twitter trolling. See, if they insult Thai royalty the way they abuse Donald Trump, they'd get a prison stretch under Section 112 of the Thai Criminal Code, which says, "Whoever defames, insults or threatens the King, the Queen, the Heir-apparent or the Regent, shall be punished with imprisonment of three to fifteen years."

Maybe Japan? You'd be lucky to get beyond border control—in 2016 the country accepted just 0.3 percent of refugee applicants, which is no accident. Japan wants to protect its culture as it sees fit, which is fine (every country is well within its rights to decide this), but let's not pretend they're better at immigration than we are. They're not.

In fact, America is the ultimate success story on immigration, despite what our critics say. According to the Department of Homeland Security, a total of 1,127,167 immigrants obtained legal permanent status in 2017. That's up from 720,177 in 1995. And as of 2015, the total number of immigrants in the United States was 47 million. Out of a country of 327 million, that's nearly 15 percent. If we're xenophobic, we're not very good at it.

OK, how about Sweden? That's the country every left-winger tells you is the model for what America should be. Well, that's fine, except the population is primarily white, which sounds pretty racist by the left's ridiculous rules. Oh, and since they've welcomed large numbers of African migrants, Sweden has struggled with assimilation and is now the rape capital of Europe.

I suppose Switzerland or Norway are alternative options, but the cost of living in these places is sky-high, which would force many Americans back into the working-class bracket while the rich live it up. Hardly the socialist vision people are calling for.

France is no better. Once the cultural capital of Europe, it's now suffering under the leadership of globalist Emmanuel Macron. As I write this, Paris has witnessed months of "yellow vest" protests over rising fuel taxes—and they look set to continue.

So if none of these places are better than America, where else could our woke celebrities go—the seventy-plus countries that outlaw homosexuality, such as Zambia, Indonesia, or Morocco? Or the many places that operate under Sharia law, which can see people stoned to death for adultery?

They could take their pick from: Afghanistan, Egypt, Iran, Iraq, Malaysia, Nigeria, Pakistan, Qatar, Saudi Arabia, Sudan, United Arab Emirates, and Yemen (although they'd have to dress modestly and know their place as women, which means minimal freedoms and male chaperones—even for a trip to the mall).

Which brings me to my next point . . .

YES, CAPITALISM IS GOOD

Indeed, America is a capitalist country and that's a good thing! As you probably know from watching *The Rubin Report*, I like to define terms, so let's actually spell out what capitalism is, because so many people seem to be confused . . .

The standard dictionary definition of capitalism is "an economic and political system in which a country's trade and industry are controlled by private owners for profit, rather than by the state."

It's also the thing that has provided you with all of the luxuries I mentioned earlier, such as the car you drive and the organic Starbucks coffee you're drinking right now.

Yes, some people are more successful in the capitalist market than others, but that's called healthy competition. What's crucial is that these people all have the same opportunity to be entrepreneurial, which they do. They can work as hard as they want for as much of the pie as they can get, or they can choose not to and that's OK too. Capitalism puts the onus on each individual to live the way he or she sees fit.

Plus, one company's success can often elevate others. A brilliant example of this is Amazon. Its existence hasn't necessarily crushed small businesses into oblivion. In many cases it has allowed independent, small-scale traders to sell via Amazon's platform, which has opened up a whole new market for them.

Yet, in true leftist style, Alexandria Ocasio-Cortez stopped Amazon from relocating to New York after scrapping any potential tax breaks. In her socialist view, Amazon is big business and big business is inherently evil, so the deal had to be upended.

The upshot of her pretzel logic? The loss of twenty-five thousand high-paying prospective jobs in the New York area.

This brings us to another point. The alternative to free-market capitalism is to live under a socialist government, which rations what we're allowed to have in terms of clothes, food, and property. Do you really trust bureaucrats to make these personal decisions for you? If so, here's some free advice: rather than trying to change the fundamental nature of our country, perhaps you should go somewhere where your (flawed) ideal already exists. See above—I just gave you a couple options. Book now on expedia.com!

ASIAN PRIVILEGE

Of course, when the woke class speaks of capitalism it claims it props up a system of white, male oppression. But this is also manufactured nonsense.

If it were true, then why do Asian Americans outperform every other ethnic group in every meaningful category in which we judge success? They're the best educated, the highest earners, and they live the longest.

According to the 2018 U.S. Census Bureau as reported in *The Wall Street Journal*, the average household income for Asian Americans was $78,000, compared with $62,000 for whites, $46,000 for Hispanics, and $37,000 for blacks.

This isn't likely to change anytime soon, with Asian Americans more likely to have a bachelor's degree than any other race in the country.

Of course, this isn't necessarily a bad thing. It's actually very impressive when you consider that most first-generation Asians moved here with very little (just like virtually everyone else) and worked their way up, showing that the American dream is based on merit, not melanin.

Despite this, Harvard University has chosen to make it harder for Asian applicants to be accepted into the university because they outperform their peers. So yes, systemic racism is real . . . at America's top university.

Speaking of skin color . . .

STOP BEING RACIST AND SEXIST—
TO STRAIGHT WHITE MEN

I never thought I'd be writing this, but fifty years on from Martin Luther King's historic "I Have a Dream" speech, it's now fashionable to judge people based on skin color and gender—if they're straight white men.

People argue this is reverse racism, but I disagree. As far as I'm concerned, it's just good old-fashioned racism.

The same goes for sexism. Thinking men are wrong or evil, simply because they are men, is just as bad as saying women belong pregnant and in the kitchen.

The simple truth is that white men are (largely) the architects of modern-day America—which, by the way, is totally fine. Without them we would be a much lesser country.

Don't believe me? See for yourself. From Thomas Jefferson's Declaration of Independence to Abraham Lincoln's ending of slavery, it's pasty white dudes who've enshrined your ability to hate them.

They're also the majority of the guys who fought in every single American war since time began, not to mention the people who built your roads, bridges, hospitals, and schools.

Reality check: They didn't do this as a vanity project in the name of white maleness. Many of them were just working to feed their family and inadvertently built civilization on the side. THEY JUST HAPPENED TO BE MALE AND WHITE!

Of course, mainstream culture won't honor this truth—but you, as a freethinker, should. People who buy into hating white men are prime examples of what Friedrich Nietzsche (another white man) referred to when he said: "Whoever fights monsters should see to it that in the process he does not become a monster. And if you gaze long enough into an abyss, the abyss will gaze back into you."

In other words, today's progressives have now become the sexists and racists they've claimed to hate.

Through the Intersectional Matrix of Lunacy, they've bought into victimhood culture—and now feel justified in hating their "oppressor." Except, they're all wrong. None of them are oppressed. They've been sold a lie.

Just look at how easy it is for me to sell a vision of an evil matriarchy that would leave men justified in hating women: Men don't have equal parenting rights. They live much shorter lives because of a life expectancy gap. Men are a minority on college campuses, and are told to "believe all women."

See what I did there? Clearly, we must take down this oppressive sisterhood. Someone please open an Etsy shop and sell *The Future Is Male* T-shirts!

OK, now that you can appreciate how ridiculous victimhood mentality is, there's absolutely nothing stopping you from getting off your ass and changing your world. Not your race, sexuality, age, class, or gender.

Yes, the system loves to spin you a different narrative, but that's what I'm here for. To give you truth bombs. So let me blow up that myth right now. If you work hard and are nice to people, nobody will give a flying fuck about your sexuality, your race, your gender, or whether you're an atheist, polysexual vegan with blue hair. Seriously.

Nothing is holding you or anyone else back. Especially not straight white men.

Not only are minorities some of the most famous and success-ful players in Hollywood, they are also among the most powerful people in our country's leading industries. Take, for instance, openly gay CEO of Apple Tim Cook (net worth $500 million); female CEO of YouTube Susan Wojcicki (net worth $500 million); and CEO of General Motors Mary Barra (net worth $60 million).

This is part of why Jay-Z (a black man, in case you'd forgotten) is now hip-hop's first billionaire and why Rihanna (a black immigrant from Barbados) was recently named the world's richest female musi-cian with a wealth of $600 million.

The same goes for Ellen DeGeneres—America's favorite lesbian—who's paid a salary of $77 million and is one of TV's top earners. In addition to this, there's Judge Judith Sheindlin, aka Judge Judy, who happens to earn $147 million per year. Not bad for a little old Jewish lady.

Last, but not least, there's Oprah Winfrey, who's managed to become a one-woman media empire with an estimated fortune of $2.5 billion.

The astounding success of these minorities was all enabled through a complicated mix of hard work, good fortune, freedom, capitalism, and opportunity. All of the above success stories come from vastly different backgrounds (Oprah grew up in an abusive household surrounded by total poverty, for example), but they've all achieved the American dream.

That's because, unlike the modern left, the American dream does not discriminate.

Ask yourself: If it did, then how could each of these aforemen-tioned people become so wildly successful and influential? Why is black culture so wholly embraced across music, film, and TV by today's youth? Why was Childish Gambino's music video for "This Is America" watched more than 120 million times in ten days—and then dubbed a cultural phenomenon? Only in America can someone earn millions of dollars making art about how racist America is. What a country!

I'll tell you why. It's because of the United States. The land of the free that allows self-expression, the pursuit of ambition, and a truly open, diverse model. Accept this graciously and use it as a force for good, rather than getting fat and lazy on the comforts that were hard-earned by people before you.

Besides, even if none of this were true—which it is—America would still be the greatest country in the universe. Why? Because we created *Seinfeld*, Bubble Wrap, and turducken.

Seriously, what's not to love?

Realizing there's almost nothing not to love, the left invents problems to fill the void. In the next chapter, you'll learn how to spot it when these lies manifest in mainstream news.

8

Learn How to Spot Fake News

SHOULD PROBABLY thank the mainstream media.

If it weren't for their abject failure to do their jobs, you'd have no idea who I was. I'd probably be back doing stand-up in comedy clubs or out of the business altogether.

My (increasingly demonetized) YouTube channel would have no reason to exist, my (frequently shadowbanned) Twitter account would be utterly irrelevant, and instead of reading this book, you'd be engrossed in the latest offering from J. K. Rowling: *Harry Potter and the Vegan Millennials of Unspecified Gender.*

My garage would also be just like everyone else's—a place for the lawn mower, old tennis rackets, and childhood memorabilia—rather than a TV studio.

Alas, the people in charge keep lying to you, so they leave me with no choice but to do my thing. Hey, I'm no journalist, but someone's got to be the designated adult in the room.

So, if this were my Pulitzer Prize acceptance speech, I'd have to thank my manager, my agent, and all those at networks MSNBC,

CNN, and ABC for their complete lack of impartiality. Great job, guys! You each made it happen in your own special way.

Then I'd need to praise each of the columnists at *The New York Times*, *The Washington Post*, *The Los Angeles Times*, and *The Guardian*, who've worked tirelessly to avoid facts that might contradict their narratives. It's exhausting work, but somebody's gotta do it!

Last, but not least, there's the "journalists" at *Salon*, *The Daily Beast*, *Vox*, and *BuzzFeed*, who've all swapped serious reporting for millennial activism. Without their collective efforts, I'd be way less successful, so big thanks to all of them.

But really, putting my mild exaggerations aside, the media truly is a cabal of hyperpartisan, habitual liars who are destroying an entire industry from within.

They're also drunk with power, hold contempt for the general public, and are willing to abuse their platforms to further a left-wing agenda.

It took me years to accept this depressing fact. Nobody wants to believe they're being manipulated, much less by the media, which is supposed to be the safeguard of the U.S. republic.

Basically, until you see this truth, you're living like Truman Burbank—Jim Carrey's character in *The Truman Show* movie; blissfully unaware that outsiders are pulling the strings of your life for their benefit.

But it wasn't always like this.

For decades in America, since the early days of television, we had three prime-time network news programs: ABC, NBC, and CBS. They all basically reported on the same issues, with very little difference. People often watched one over the other simply according to which news anchor they happened to like more. Each network probably had its own unique bias, but they weren't as overt and obvious.

Yes, this limited the totality of the news we got, but all of us basically received the same information, which was presented to us by people who'd long held ethical journalistic standards.

Then, in 1980, Ted Turner changed the game with his news network, CNN, which broadcasted 24-7. With more time to dedicate to real stories and more resources to spend on reporting news around the globe, the world got a little bigger for the American viewer.

Throughout the next thirty years, CNN journalists did some incredible, groundbreaking reporting. I remember watching them in the morning before school in the fall of 1990 as they reported live from Kuwait during the Gulf War. Even though I was only in ninth grade, I knew it was something important and something real. Journalists on the ground in another country during a war. It was the first time I had seen that in my lifetime.

CNN also was by far the best in the aftermath of the 9/11 attacks. Like everyone else, I was glued to my television in the days and weeks that followed, which was surreal because I was living in the very city in which the largest attack occurred.

This period saw the explosion of cable news, and suddenly CNN faced competition on the right and on the left from Fox News and MSNBC. Each had debuted in 1996, but after 9/11 they all became household names. Since then, these cable news networks have jockeyed for ratings with an endless array of hosts, formats, and shows designed to keep you angry and outraged depending on the direction of your politics.

Of course, all that anger and outrage is nothing compared with what has been birthed online with the advent of digital journalism in the 2000s.

Almost overnight, trusted sources (who were invited into our homes via the TV screen) were competing with random bloggers and vloggers of all descriptions, many of whom had no dealings with proofreaders, fact-checkers, or copy editors. What they were good at, though, was keeping people clicking from story to story by talking directly to camera and using catchy graphics and jump cuts to make the news seem more fun and off the cuff. The amateurishness of it all often added to its credibility because audiences had begun to see through the stiff network veneer.

To survive, commercial stations began creating content with equal speed and ferocity, often preying on their viewers' emotions (perpetual outrage, sadness) rather than on facts and neutrality. Consequently, quality control fell by the wayside.

Over time this manipulation by media phased out traditional reporting and created the hysterical attention deficit disorder–inducing news we have today.

Not that technology is solely to blame, of course. Technology is just a tool, and it's up to us humans whether to use that tool for good or evil.

College professors who've infused the curriculum with progressive politics have also contributed to this dereliction of duties. Once upon a time they schooled journalism majors in the technical aspects of the job, but now they frame everything in left-wing politics. This mass brainwashing is hugely effective too. Newsrooms are now filled with progressive activists who bend the truth, as opposed to old-school professionals who feel a duty to both themselves and their audience.

Don't believe me? Even CBS's Lara Logan admitted that journalists have become political activists.

"Eighty-five percent of journalists are registered Democrats," she told the *Mike Drop Podcast*.

> How do you know you're being lied to? How do you know you're being manipulated? How do you know there's something not right with the coverage? When they simplify it all [and] there's no gray. It's all one way. Well, life isn't like that. If it doesn't match real life, it's probably not.
>
> When you turn on your computer, or you walk past the TV, or you see a newspaper headline in the grocery store. If they're all saying the same thing, the weight of that convinces you that it's true. You don't question it, because everyone is saying it.
>
> Although the media has historically always been left-leaning, we've abandoned our pretense—or at least the effort—to be objective today. We've become political activists, and some could argue propagandists.

So there you have it, a journalist sick of "journalists." Logan bravely acknowledging what so many of us instinctively know to be true after so many years of being lied to.

Don't take my word for it though; let's look back at three of the biggest media hit jobs carried out in the past few years.

We all remember the Covington scandal of January 2019. This event saw a group of Kentucky high school students (yep, minors) wrongfully accused of racially harassing an elderly Native American, Nathan Phillips.

The now infamous footage of one of the boys standing face-to-face with the man outside the Lincoln Memorial in Washington D.C. was spun to make it seem that a group of students wearing MAGA hats were racially harassing an innocent victim. This intended bias perfectly fit the media narrative that Trump supporters are racist, thus the incident exploded on both mainstream and social media.

BOYS IN MAGA HATS MOB NATIVE ELDER, declared *The New York Times*, while CNN baited viewers with TEENS MOCKING NATIVE AMERICAN ELDER IGNITES OUTRAGE.

The Washington Post was no better. It followed suit with its own creative writing, titled "NATIVE AMERICAN SPEAKS ON THE MAGA-HAT-WEARING TEENS WHO SURROUNDED HIM."

This report relied almost completely on the one-sided testimony of Phillips, claiming he'd served in Vietnam (he hadn't) and that one of the boys shouted "build that wall" (he hadn't). It also featured impassioned statements from the Indigenous Peoples Movement, which diagnosed it as "emblematic of our discourse in Trump's America."

As I watched this all unfold, I knew there had to be more to the story. So, while the Twitter mob assembled, I waited for more information. Sure, this meant I would have to pass up on thousands of retweets and likes, but that's just how strong my moral courage is. Not all heroes wear capes.

In reality, it eventually turned out that it was the Covington boys themselves who were the victims in the confrontation. They were in D.C. for a March for Life rally to support the pro-life position. While peacefully assembling, they were heckled by a group of Black Hebrew Israelites, who referred to them as "faggots" and "incest babies."

When Phillips got in their faces, one of the boys—sixteen-year-old Nick Sandmann—stood motionless and smirked as he tried to defuse the tension. A full-length video proved this, but it was already too late. The Twitterati narrative was already out there. White, privileged, antiwoman Christians were the bad guys and an elderly Native American was the good guy. (The racist Black Israelites were largely ignored because the fact that they were yelling "faggots" at the kids would've thrown a major wrench into the intersectional machinery.)

The students and their parents received death threats and the school was forced to close down over security fears. Still, the mainstream press didn't relent. Its propaganda was getting clicks, selling papers, and boosting its narrative, which all translates to money and power.

The Washington Post's Jonathan Capehart—a member of the paper's editorial board—fueled this outrage when he wrote an opinion piece stating: "Ask just about anyone who is not straight, white and male what they see in that smirk and you'll most likely open up a world of hurt. Memories of continual bullying and other abuse at the hands of entitled men and boys who never feared being held accountable."

Then the paper's fashion critic, Robin Givhan, described all MAGA hats as "an inflammatory declaration of identity." And so it continued.

Noah Berlatsky wrote a piece for NBC titled, A STUDENT AT COVINGTON CATHOLIC SAYS HE WAS A SILENT BYSTANDER IN VIRAL VIDEO. BUT HIS MAGA HAT SPOKE FOR HIM, while *Vulture*'s Erik Abriss said, "I just want these people to die. Simple as that. Every single one of them. And their parents."

Oh my, the progressive tolerance is just endless, isn't it?

Eventually, the press were forced to backpedal when lawyers came calling with multimillion-dollar lawsuits, but this capitulation happened reluctantly and without apology or retraction. Many of their tweets remain, like this one from former CNN host Reza Aslan, who posted a picture of Sandmann along with the caption: "Honest question. Have you ever seen a more punchable face than this kid's?"

I assure you, conservatives have been banned from Twitter for much less.

This twist of reality was capped by *The Today Show*'s Savannah Guthrie, who interviewed Sandmann at his home and suggested that he should apologize.

Given Sandmann's lawsuits remain active—totaling more than $500 million—you'd think the press might've learned something from this embarrassing episode, but nope, they persevere.

The same month as the Covington fiasco, the media found another case that was just too good to be true (as they always are). This time it was a hate crime against gay, black actor Jussie Smollett, who told police he'd been attacked outside his Chicago apartment by two men shouting, "This is MAGA country," who then "tied a noose around his neck and poured bleach on his skin."

Instantly, the media were obsessed. Every left-wing TV channel dedicated rolling coverage to the story and exercised little or no caution when reporting it, even though the actor wasn't seriously injured and there was no corroborating evidence to support the details of the case, which appeared sketchy right from the beginning.

None of this mattered. No progressive journalist bothered to fact-check or dig deeper into the specifics. Instead, they amplified the feelings of Democrat senator Cory Booker of New Jersey, who didn't wait to hail the incident as "a modern-day attempted lynching."

Unsurprisingly, the hits kept coming from Democrats on Twitter, who now had an incident that could tell a story they so deeply wanted to be true.

Bernie Sanders hailed it as proof of the "surging hostility towards minorities around the country." Nancy Pelosi called it "an affront to our humanity." And congresswoman Maxine Waters said she was "dedicated to finding the culprits and bringing them to justice."

Meanwhile, Andrew Cuomo, the governor of New York, said: "New York State calls this attack on Jussie Smollett exactly what it is—a hate crime."

ABC's Robin Roberts then conducted an hour-long interview with Smollett even while the story was falling apart, but she failed to ask a single probing question, taking everything he said as gospel instead. (Personally, I always try to give interviewers the longest leash possible, and know we all have our own styles, but Roberts either dropped the ball here or intentionally didn't address the growing issues around Smollett's story.)

According to the headlines, pundits, and politicians, America had finally been exposed as a hotbed of white supremacy. Except, much to their dismay, the whole incident turned out to be a giant hoax. On February 20, 2019, Smollett was charged with filing a fake police report and accused of paying two Nigerian brothers to orchestrate the "attack."

Yup, America is just so absolutely fantastic, and capitalism is just so spectacularly great, that a rich actor who once would've had to hire a publicist to get into the press instead hires immigrant brothers to pretend to beat him up. It not only fits the mainstream narrative, but you'll save a bunch on the publicist!

When the hoax became too obvious to ignore, the media refused to admit they had been duped. Instead, they doubled down on their behavior.

The Washington Post responded with the op-ed, I DOUBTED JUSSIE SMOLLETT. IT BREAKS MY HEART THAT I MIGHT BE RIGHT, while CNN's Brian Stelter—host of the most ironically named TV show in history, *Reliable Sources*—claimed the network had done "careful reporting" on the case, despite the fact that his CNN colleague Ryan Young had declared the incident a "racist and homophobic assault" before police could investigate.

Once again, the press refused to hold itself accountable and pretended nothing happened. This is one of the advantages of keeping everyone outraged all the time. When you realize how the media has misled you, it's already sent you down another rabbit hole of its choosing.

These two cases, Covington and Smollett, were both unfolding at the same time as the Russian collusion theory—a drama that ran for two years largely thanks to MSNBC's Rachel Maddow, who was desperate to convince her viewers of election-rigging with the Kremlin.

She, like many of her media cohorts, ran countless hours of coverage on the conspiracy theory that Donald Trump had somehow stolen the 2016 election with help from Russian officials. Every day was about a new theory, a new email exposed, and a new secret meeting that had taken place.

The media's partisanship got so nuts that *The New Yorker* printed one of their covers in Russian.

When the multimillion-dollar Special Counsel investigation headed by Robert Mueller was later dropped in April 2019, vindicating the president, there was no apology—just more doubling down.

"We are not investigators," said CNN's president, Jeff Zucker. "We are journalists, and our role is to report the facts as we know them, which is exactly what we did."

The New York Times's executive editor, Dean Baquet, was equally duplicitous. "We wrote a lot about Russia, and I have no regrets," he said. "It's not our job to determine whether or not there was illegality."

Just take a moment to appreciate the confusion of these two statements. At the most base level both men do make a point that the job of a journalist is to report facts and not to judge their illegality or not. This is true. But what they obfuscate is that it's their responsibility to focus on where the facts actually are, and not to chase down only the facts that fit their narratives. If, however, you watched CNN or read *The New York Times* during the two years encompassing the Russia Hoax, you know that ignoring the facts of the matter is exactly what these media did. They remain unapologetic about serving you a diet of fake news because they're so blinded by the profits that their political tribalism reaps. Sure, virtually everything they reported about regarding Mueller's #Russiagate and Smollett's #HateHoax turned out to be false, but apparently that's just reporters doing their job.

So with their own shoddy definition of journalism in mind, why would you want to give them any of your time or money?

The annual cost of *The New York Times* delivery to your home can be $532, which could be better spent on countless other things, such as feeding hungry children, avoiding foreclosure on your home, or throwing quarters into a fountain.

I had this conversation recently with my father, who's been a loyal subscriber to *The New York Times* for more than three decades and is finally considering scrapping his subscription after the newspaper did a hatchet job on me in a cover story titled "The Making of a YouTube Radical."

In it, "journalist" Kevin Roose cites a young man, Caleb Cain, who watches conservative YouTube content and suddenly flirts with neo-Nazism.

The June 2019 article (which included a montage of YouTubers on the front page) blamed me, plus a host of others, including podcast host Joe Rogan and commentator Philip DeFranco, for radicalizing a generation into disliking women, gays, and blacks—you know the drill.

The piece even managed to include a picture of Milton Friedman, free-market economist. (In 1976, Friedman was awarded the Sveriges Riksbank Prize in Economic Sciences in memory of Alfred Nobel! Quite a racist, that guy.)

"I've heard countless versions of Mr. Cain's story: an aimless young man—usually white, frequently interested in video games—visits YouTube looking for direction or distraction and is seduced by a community of far-right creators," Roose wrote.

"Some travel all the way to neo-Nazism, while others stop at milder forms of bigotry."

Conveniently, the article was released just as *Vox* "journalist" Carlos Maza (the same guy who pressured Democrat politician Pete Buttigieg not to do my show) lobbied YouTube into censoring conservatives over a spat with comedian Steven Crowder.

A cynic might think this was a coordinated attack, especially when Roose used his article to state: "YouTube has created a dangerous on-ramp to extremism by combining two things: a business model that rewards provocative videos with exposure and advertising dollars, and an algorithm that guides users down personalized paths meant to keep them glued to their screens."

Clearly Roose has never seen any of my dozens, if not hundreds, of tweets to @TeamYouTube in which I implore them to stop unsubscribing people from my channel or deflating its view count. The idea that my channel is radicalizing people, or keeping viewers in a click-hole, is simply absurd.

Unsurprisingly, Roose's article fell apart from the very beginning. Soon after the story went live, he was forced to clarify that many of those pictured in the article weren't, in fact, far right.

"This collage is just a sample from his viewing history. Some far right, some not," Roose said, responding to criticism. When pushed to correct it, he added: "I hear you. Working on it."

Hours later, little had changed. "We've updated the collage with a caption to explain that it's a sample of videos that Caleb watched. We're also tweaking how the grid fades so it's clearer that people like DeFranco are not far right."

The only reason that Roose mildly conceded and *The New York Times* issued the caption was because people like me, Shapiro, and DeFranco have enough of a social media following to hit back. (Ironically, this is also the very reason that hit pieces are written about us in the first place. We've grown too powerful outside of the mainstream institutions.)

Despite the minor correction, the damage had been done. DeFranco and Shapiro were still on the cover of the print edition of

The New York Times in an article about far-right radicalization, and my picture had been moved a couple pages in, above the headline MAKING OF A YOUTUBE RADICAL: ALGORITHMS AND THE ALT-RIGHT.

Soon after, Roose went on CNN to promote his work, but still refused to engage with any of the people he'd written about, including me.

I repeatedly invited Roose on *The Rubin Report* to explain his cover story. After ignoring me for a week, despite thousands of retweets and interactions, he declined, responding, "I'm good, thanks!" before adding that I have a "fascinating booking strategy"—snide posts that were Liked by various members of the left-wing press, including CNN's Oliver Darcy, *NYT*'s Mat Yurow, NPR's Ben Bergman, *The Guardian*'s Siva Vaidhyanathan, and the *LA Times*' Jeff Bercovici.

I don't care about any of these people specifically, but their actions point to exactly why the media is so distrusted: An activist writes an arguably libelous article. Then one of the subjects of the article invites the author to discuss said article. The author then declines and is lauded by his own community as a righteous defender of truth.

Owning truth is pretty easy when you can say what you want without ever having to defend yourself.

Twitter behavior aside though, Roose's article undermined itself from the beginning.

The article's entire premise—that Cain was radicalized by YouTube promoting conservative content—was totally debunked by the conclusion to the article itself, which stated Cain ended up watching far-left content.

Yes, that's right. The article about YouTube radicalizing people to the far right ends with the subject becoming a lefty. You can't make this shit up.

Cain also later admitted that he had never considered himself "alt right" anyway, so *The New York Times* fabricated a narrative in yet another attempt to intimidate YouTube into deplatforming creators.

These three examples combined (which are just a drop in the bucket) help explain why trust in mainstream media is at an all-time low.

According to a 2018 poll by the Gallup and Knight Foundation, the overwhelming majority of Americans distrust the media. Specifically, 90 percent of Republicans, 75 percent of independents, and 66 percent of moderates.

Nearly a third of these people said their distrust was permanent.

So, with this in mind, how can you possibly navigate the media more consciously? I get asked this question everywhere I go. And unfortunately the onus is now on you. The only answer is to work harder for the truth.

But how? First, it helps to know what fake news actually is. Back in 2016, *Rubin Report* guest (and the man who coined the term *Intellectual Dark Web*) Eric Weinstein broke it down into four categories: narrative-driven, algorithmic, institutional, and blatant falsehoods.

- Narrative-driven is basically a foregone conclusion that's presented as inevitable. The media epitome was probably *Newsweek*'s "Madam President" cover, which was ready to hit the printers weeks before anybody even voted in the 2016 election. Editors clearly predicted the outcome and actively worked toward that assumption, rather than being neutral and open to all eventualities.

- Algorithmic describes how social media manipulates our news intake based on whatever we've previously clicked. This might sound OK, like it's tailor-made for our benefit, but it skews reality by editing the landscape. Back in the day, this was called "burying the lead"— aka de-emphasizing a story we dislike by putting it on page 18, rather than the front cover. Again, this isn't helpful, because news isn't something we should view according to what's "nice." It should be based on what's necessary.
- Institutional fake news is where a highly respected organization, such as MIT or Harvard, releases a study and passes it off as objective fact. These examples get little pushback from reporters because it's usually difficult to disagree with academic experts on their technical data. (And often the journalists don't want to put in the effort to read the reports in the first place. They take the conclusion as fact and run with it.)
- Lastly, blatant falsehoods are exactly that—outright lies. These can stem from a teenage blogger's bedroom or a high-powered publicist's spin room. Either way, it doesn't matter. Once they're published, it's hard to correct the falsehood.

So now that you know these types of fake news, test what you see against this checklist and consume it with a fresh perspective.

Curating a list of trusted journalists will also help. This doesn't have to be static—it can change over time—but you'll want people who generally operate in good faith.

To ensure this is their motive, check their output. Does it always reach the same conclusion? Does their criticism only flow in one direction? If so, take a step back. Reporters should be conduits for information, not manipulators of it.

Here's another tip: don't let yourself exist in an echo chamber. Seeing the wider scope of headlines from across the spectrum will help you view information in a broader context, diluting the risk of forming any single bias.

You should also rely on gut instinct. As humans, we evolved with this unconscious intuition to better survive the wilds of nature while hunting for food. Now we need it to get through the day without being manipulated by bad actors and crumbling institutions. So if you sense that something's amiss, delve deeper. Go to the original source and check it for yourself. Yeah, it's work, but that's life.

Books are another remedy. Trust me, they usually take much longer to produce, cover subjects in greater depth, and must get past a team of eagle-eyed editors. All these qualities help to make books far more robust and reliable than a listicle written in twenty minutes and published on *BuzzFeed*.

Of course, there's always an element of risk to all of this, but it's one of the only ways to exercise quality control without living under a rock.

More than anything else though, think critically about the issues of the day. Just because *The New York Times*'s slogan is "All the news that's fit to print" doesn't mean that is really the case. Just because CNN promotes itself as "the most trusted name in news" doesn't mean that is actually a fact.

News is a business like any other. Although we'd like to think that the business it's in is to inform and enlighten, we should always remember that it's really in the business of keeping our eyes on the TV or our fingers clicking. Just because someone has good hair and sits behind a well-lit desk doesn't mean the person is an authority on anything. (Except, perhaps, on how to get a job in cable TV.)

So when a story seems to be too good to be true because it fits the world exactly as you see it, remember, it probably is.

And when a politician says something in a seven-second audio clip that is exactly what you'd expect them to say, realize that it was probably clipped from a much larger context. Really think about who is serving you the news and why they're delivering it in the first place. At a time when everyone's a journalist, you need to be an editor.

And if all this is too much work for you, or if you're still confused, watch the 1976 classic film *Network* to really understand why newscaster Howard Beale, played by Peter Finch, who won an Oscar for this role, was mad as hell and not gonna take it anymore. The end of his legendary speech might just be the wake-up call you need:

> So, I want you to get up now. I want all of you to get up out of your chairs. I want you to get up right now and go to the window. Open it, and stick your head out, and yell: "I'm as mad as hell, and I'm not gonna take this anymore!"
>
> I want you to get up right now. Sit up. Go to your windows. Open them up and stick your head out and yell—"I'm as mad as hell and I'm not gonna take this anymore!" Things have got to change. But first, you've gotta get mad! . . . You've got to say, "I'm as mad as hell, and I'm not gonna take this anymore!"

9

Find a Mentor

B Y JANUARY 2018, my successes and failures had added up to be a net positive. I was finally doing work that I was truly proud of.

This included connecting with viewers from all over the world—many of whom sent messages of support. From the United States and Canada, to India and Pakistan, to Sweden and Norway, people all over the world were appreciative of my defense of free speech through the conversations I was having.

One thing that consistently amazed me was that it wasn't just emails or Twitter DMs (direct messages) that people were sending, but handwritten letters, often pages in length, in which people would tell me their life stories couched around their own political wake-up, which had something to do with me.

Many heartfelt letters were from conservatives, who said they'd never seen a New York "liberal" discuss their views without belittling and demeaning them, and disaffected liberals also praised my willingness to defend free speech against the barrage of crazy hostility from their own side.

The letters (in whichever form they arrived) were (and remain) a constant source of inspiration for me to this day. How unbelievably inspiring that a middle-aged woman in Paris is thinking the same thing as a college student in India and an American expat living in Kuwait.

There were times we'd get calls from the post office because our PO box was overflowing with letters and packages. Fans would often share their gratitude by sending pieces of art, which they'd spent weeks or months creating by hand.

Ironically, all too often these people would ask me not to publicly credit or identify their work for fear that they'd be attacked online for supporting me. Really think about that for a moment. I'd sparked something in someone that inspired art, and with a simple tweet, I could direct business their way. But, in fear of the endless outrage mob (the very thing they respect me for fighting), they'd often ask me not to give them public credit.

I totally get it, and at an individual level I respect their decision and would never betray their trust, but if there ever was a microcosm of the problem here, this was it.

Bravery was in shortage. I was becoming a brave-person proxy for people who felt they had too much to lose. But if I thought I was affecting things, boy was I in for a big surprise.

A six-foot three-inch Canadian psychologist was about to show me how it's really done . . .

Dr. Jordan Peterson was appearing on *The Rubin Report* as part of a special episode with Ben Shapiro. Although our circles had all been moving closer and closer, this was the first time they'd both been seen together on camera, and I was very aware of the relevance and importance. Neither of them asked for topics beforehand, but I wanted to cover new ground with each and see where the points of agreement and disagreement were. We talked about everything from politics and religion to the nature of reality itself. I've never asked Ben this, but I wonder if that conversation ultimately led him to write his latest book, *The Right Side of History*, which dived deeply into these very topics.

I knew the livestream would catch fire on YouTube, but the finished product surpassed even my expectations—it attracted five million views on YouTube and millions more on our audio podcast. We went for two hours without a break and only ended because Jordan was booked to do his first live stage show. He was scheduled to appear at the Orpheum Theatre in downtown Los Angeles later that evening.

I knew Jordan would've kept talking for as long as we would've kept the lights on, but I wanted to be respectful of his time and make sure that he was rested up enough for his big event.

As we wrapped, Ben bolted as quickly as he talks, because, of course, he too had another engagement to get to. As Jordan was collecting his things I casually quipped, "Hey, if you need someone to warm up the crowd with a few lobster jokes tonight, let me know."

Obviously, I wasn't seriously suggesting a creative partnership—after all, who the hell would invite themselves onto somebody else's tour just hours before it was set to begin?—but, without missing a beat, he replied, "Absolutely! That sounds like a great idea. Come on down. I'll see you later."

The front door closed behind him and, like a scene from *Curb Your Enthusiasm*, I stood there, slack-jawed. What had I gotten myself into?

I'd only done stand-up a handful of times since moving to L.A. five years earlier, and I'd never performed in a real theater in front of three thousand people who were there for some serious self-help.

Excited, albeit a little unprepared, I reassured myself that it was just a one-off gig to enjoy. It wasn't as if I was about to embark on a yearlong international tour with the greatest intellectual of our time. Right?

A couple hours later my fears were allayed as I crushed it despite having never told any of the jokes before. (I was also absolutely shocked that after the public announcer said, "And now welcome the host of *The Rubin Report*, Dave Rubin," the audience, which didn't even know I was going to be there, went absolutely bananas and gave me a standing ovation before I had even said or done anything.)

As luck would have it, the tour managers from Creative Artists Agency, better known as CAA, the most influential agency in town, were backstage for the event. Although they were there just to see if this kooky professor could even pull off a show of this magnitude, they immediately grabbed me when I left the stage and asked if I had representation.

Yadda yadda yadda, days later I signed with them, and suddenly I was about to embark on an epic trip throughout Europe, America, and Australia with the Michael Jordan of psychology. If that would make me Scottie Pippen, I'd gladly take it.

Little did I know that the professional journey was going to pale in comparison to the personal journey I was also about to embark on.

If you think one of Jordan's ninety-minute lectures leaves people inspired, try spending a year with him in planes, trains, and automobiles. Although I didn't know it at the time, Jordan was about to pass several life lessons on to me via osmosis.

For more than one hundred shows I sat backstage, right behind the giant velvet curtains, with an incredible view of the audience from behind Jordan as he spoke to thousands in packed theaters. It was never lost on me that I had the best seat in the house every night, and not only was it free, but I was actually getting paid to be there.

As each audience absorbed his knowledge and grew into better versions of themselves, so did I. And believe it or not, so did Jordan. This was a point he made many evenings during the tour: he too was learning and noodling through topics onstage and the ideas evolved as the tour proceeded.

Other times, we'd be just out and about in a new city, and he'd demonstrate a principle, belief, or approach through his behavior or posture (yes, he always stands up straight with his shoulders back). It was obvious to me right from the get-go that the "12 Rules" weren't just some abstract ideas he put into a book, but rather lifelong lessons learned that he was incorporating into his own life. Seeing it firsthand was dislodging something in my brain in real time.

Sometimes I'd wonder, Could he possibly be the real deal? I mean, are there people who really live up to their ideals all the time?

This question sat in the back of my mind and was clearly answered one night in London. Jordan and I were invited for dinner at Douglas Murray's flat along with Maajid Nawaz. It was a *Rubin Report* reunion with all the spouses and significant others, except for my husband, David, who was back in California during that leg of the trip.

I know you'd love some juicy details of the conversation that night, and I can assure you it was a passionate debate on everything from politics to religion, but some things are better left between friends.

I mention this evening though because just as we entered the apartment, Douglas's cat was rubbing all over my leg. As someone who is super allergic to cats, I quietly prayed that it wasn't going to set off a crazy allergic reaction and cut my night short. Fortunately it didn't, and we had about four hours of food, wine, and whiskey.

As we were leaving, it hit me that at no point in the evening had I seen Jordan pet the cat, which is Rule 12, "Pet a Cat When You Encounter One on the Street." Though we were in a comfy London apartment and not on a street, it seemed that if Jordan didn't pet the cat this would be a real chink in the armor.

As we put on our coats, Jordan picked his moment, as if he had been waiting all night to do it. He kneeled down and began stroking the cat, which was now lying in his bed. They were long, comforting strokes, over and over for a solid minute. He stood up, thanked Douglas again, and we headed out.

Phew, crisis averted. The 12 Rules were still intact. The tour could go on!

This was just one of many instances in which I saw Jordan put the 12 Rules into action in his own life. Keen to remember these moments of insight, I would write them down in the back of the trusty notebook that I kept in my jacket pocket, or enter them into the Notes app on my iPhone, something I could go back to whenever I needed them.

At the time, I had no intention to ever share these moments with anyone. They were private scribblings and would stay that way. But as time passed, I realized they were universal truths that could benefit others, not just myself.

One day toward the end of our travels, Jordan reminded me that every person who gets his or her act together—even just a little bit—has the capacity to spread it around, like a chain reaction, and immeasurably improve the universe.

I guess this is my intention here. Whatever I learned during this time, I'm paying it forward for others to benefit from.

So while the Lobster Man himself has already given you his 12 Rules for Life, here are a few additional tips to help you along the way.

They worked for me, so they might just work for you too.

STOP BEING AN "EXPERT" ON EVERYTHING

Jordan Peterson is as well read, intellectually curious, and academically rigorous as I can possibly imagine anyone to be.

He's taught psychology at Harvard University—one of the world's most coveted academic institutions—and he's been a tenured professor at the University of Toronto and penned the mighty *Maps for Meaning: The Architecture of Belief*, a book that even he admits is not for the average reader.

He is universally revered—and feared—for his incredible intellect and emotional insight.

And yet he's still able to say the following words: "I don't know."

It's a pretty simple phrase, yet it remains one of the most underrated and rarely used in modern discourse. When is the last time you heard a politician say it? It pretty much never happens (though it should be noted they all suddenly say "I don't remember" when questions about their past arise).

Take a look at Twitter whenever there is a breaking story or cultural event unfolding. Everyone, from the blue-check "journalists" to the anonymous pink anime fox, is a self-proclaimed "expert" on everything, without regard for their qualifications or life experience. In fact, it's usually the total opposite. The less people seem to know about something, the more they pontificate on it.

From the Iran deal to mental health and economics, there is no subject that the chattering classes don't profess to have an authoritative opinion about, even though—in reality—they're totally clueless.

This poses an obvious question: if someone with Jordan's résumé and reputation can be humble in the face of stuff he doesn't know, why can't everyone else?

A shrink might say they were trying to overcompensate for something. Sort of like the middle-aged man with the new, flashy convertible. He's got to be hiding something. In this case, it's the pursuit of truth.

This is why the phrase "I don't know" needs a major comeback.

During our tour dates, I'd occasionally hear Jordan say "I don't know" while addressing thousands of people in packed auditoriums, all of whom had paid good money to hear his wisdom.

For instance, during our Q and A sessions, if he was asked a question about his carnivore diet, he'd always qualify his answer by saying that he wasn't a nutritionist and only knew so much. If they wanted further information, they should see a dietitian.

If he was asked about the effectiveness of psychotropic drugs, like magic mushrooms, he would make a point of saying that the evidence about their psychological effects was inconclusive. Then he would always add, "Be wary of unearned wisdom." As a guy who's done mushrooms many times in my life and stared out into space for way too many hours, I can assure you that's the right take.

And if Jordan was asked to comment on very specific happenings in U.S. politics, he'd politely remind everyone that he's Canadian and had enough on his plate with Canadian prime minister Justin Trudeau, which always got a big laugh. Especially while in Canada.

Simply put, he felt no shame in owning his "knowledge gap" and deferring to experts.

Want to know the best part? Absolutely nobody cared that the expert didn't know everything. Nobody gasped. Nobody thought any less of him for it or demanded a refund. In fact, many found his candor refreshing.

As the tour went on, I realized that these moments of humility were something I had implemented in my own work. In fact, it was a founding principle of my (frequently criticized) interview approach. Sometimes I'd be seeking knowledge or clarity as much as the viewer at home . . . and wasn't afraid to ask for it.

But I saw the true power of that humility when it came from Jordan. Every time one of those moments happened, I could actually feel the crowd pause and take a breath with him. It's almost impossible to describe what a silent humbling moment among thousands is like. You can just feel that the energy is as raw as it is real.

The audience members were relieved by the unpretentiousness, which allowed them to see him as an imperfect human. Which is exactly what he is. And what we all are.

Here's why: If you admit that you don't know something, you no longer have the stress of lying to yourself or anyone else. You can enjoy the learning process and make it a mutual exchange of ideas. It's a gift to yourself.

It gives you room to learn something new and exciting. It opens the door to fresh information and welcomes it inside, which builds your expanse of knowledge even further.

That's the incredible irony of it all: the more you admit to not knowing, the smarter you'll actually get!

Furthermore, it's also good to be humbled occasionally. The human ego can be fragile, but it can also be way too arrogant and destructive. It can obstruct your emotional and intellectual development. A little bit of modesty can offset this hubris and make us all better human beings.

So yes, saying "I don't know" is a good thing. Bullshitting your way through life is not dignified and over time it can never really work. Eventually people see through it and then are very likely to second-guess everything else you say going forward.

Have the courage to admit when knowledge eludes you. Otherwise you'll just be a dumb person's version of a smart person. And why would anyone want to be that?

I don't know.

DRESS BETTER

Another question that often came up during our Q and A sessions was when exactly did Jordan decide to become a middle-aged male fashion icon? Usually this was asked in jest, but it was clear that his days of frumpy oversize button-downs and unkempt hair were behind him.

If you look back at Jordan's lectures on YouTube from even just a few years ago, fashion was not at the top of his list. He wore big, frumpy shirts and shapeless, pleated pants. But something changed as the tour kicked into high gear.

In the weeks before we set off, he rushed through an order for four tailored suits, complete with matching vests, cufflinks, and several pairs of brand-new shoes. He even learned how to tie a Windsor knot for maximum style.

For him, this was all part of showing the world how serious he was about his message. It was also, he later told me, a mark of respect for his audience.

Typically, I preferred to keep it a little looser. I'd wear my usual *Rubin Report* getup, which consisted of jeans, boots, a casual shirt, and a sports jacket, which I'd buy online for about $60.

It was just enough polish to look professional without being stiff. Plus, Jordan was the main event, I was the warm-up, and having a slightly different style helped to keep that distinction. After all, I was cracking jokes; he was changing lives.

It also felt comfortable. I'd worn some variation of this look for years whenever I needed to be onstage or near a camera, which allowed me to relax. This consistent look got me in the right headspace, which was good for my performance.

As soon as I'd leave the stage, however, I would quickly ditch the jacket and revert back to my weekend look—shorts or beat-up jeans, a simple T-shirt, and a baseball cap. It's the sort of clothing I grew up wearing, so why would I need to try anything else? Comfort was key, especially when I was off duty.

Jordan, on the other hand, would always maintain a certain standard, regardless of where we were, what we were doing, and how everybody else in the crew dressed.

One scorching hot day, when we were walking along a beach in Melbourne, Australia, he stepped out in a pair of light-colored trousers and a breathable button-down shirt and jacket, while I was wearing some basic T-shirt, old shorts, and flip-flops.

I didn't think much of it at first, until fans began to approach us. I'd watch them interact with him and could see that they weren't disappointed by his presence. The man in real life was the same man they'd gotten to know through his work. Even out of context—far away from a well-lit TV studio or theater stage—Jordan was still who they envisioned him to be. His outward appearance represented order and self-care, which is the essence of what he always talks about.

The external matched the internal. He was the real deal.

As we walked down the boardwalk at the beach, I asked Jordan about his uptick in personal style. It turns out it was one of his 12 Rules for Life that didn't make the final edit.

"Dress like the person you want to be," he told me. "I took it from Nietzsche. He once said 'every great man is an actor of his own ideal,' which means you have to act out whatever you want to be, then you'll become it."

It was right out of the film *Field of Dreams*: build it and they will come.

"It's not a lie," he added. "It's a form of practice. Figure out who you want to be, then dress like that person. No detail is too small to overlook. If you're at any critical point of your life, you should do everything you can to tip the scales—not in your favor, but in favor of having the right thing happen."

He was obviously correct and it's something we are all aware of every day. *Dressing well not only can determine what energy you put into the universe, but also what you get in return.*

This is why people judge books by their covers. It's why every publishing house in America, including Penguin, the publisher of this very book, has a team of designers who spend weeks creating the perfect jackets for its titles.

These designers focus on every possible facet, from font size to color and imagery. There were times during this process when I'd sit in on these meetings and feel amazed by how they could debate such small, seemingly inconsequential aspects for hours.

Should the match on the cover of this book be lit, or should it not? Should the font be bolder or thinner? Should we italicize certain words for added impact? Just take a quick look at the cover of this book and you'll see what I'm talking about. (Apologies to everyone at Penguin, especially the graphic artist, for the roughly four hundred emails I sent demanding the tiniest of changes until I felt this book cover was perfect. We really nailed it though, didn't we?)

It took me a while to appreciate this, but now I get it: These nonverbal characteristics speak to people on a sensory level. It's an indicator of what's going on inside.

The same is true of people.

Exactly one year after our first show together, Jordan and I returned to the same venue where it all began: the Orpheum Theatre in Los Angeles.

This time, I upped my game. I wore a jet-black suit by British designer Ted Baker, which was tailored for the best possible fit. I wore it with a stylish tie and a pair of fresh dress shoes. I put in the effort to look my best and I felt like a million bucks.

And you know what happened? It was perhaps the best show of the entire tour.

As if by magic, every single joke landed perfectly, the energy in the auditorium was electric, and I felt a better connection with the crowd (who, incidentally, were also pretty well-dressed themselves). I even managed to reunite Jordan with Ben Shapiro, who made a surprise guest appearance carrying a "gay" wedding cake for me. The crowd ate it up.

Dressing as the person I wanted to be—the best, sharpest, funniest version of myself—did something on a cognitive level, which then had a butterfly effect on everything else that followed.

Since then, I've made a concerted effort to improve my appearance and maximize the power it offers. Don't get me wrong—on the weekends I've still got my favorite baseball hats, jeans, and sneakers for when I'm lounging around the house, but I've also added some sharp suits, quality shirts, and fitted jackets to the mix for when the situation, the audience, and the universe deserve it.

Likewise, I get regular haircuts, manage what I eat, and exercise. Combined, it all makes a difference to how I feel, behave, and interact, because it's all connected to the self.

Don't believe me? Fine. But just take a quick look at our most vocal critics.

It's no coincidence that social justice warriors are frequently out of shape, poorly dressed, and have messy hair, along with their overall disheveled appearance. If some dress for success, they dress for failure.

Now get out there and buy yourself something nice. Your future deserves it.

ADMIT THAT WE NEED
RELIGIOUS STORIES

In 1997 I spent my spring semester studying in Israel. At the end of the school year a friend and I traveled to Sinai, a vast desert between Israel and Egypt, and the home of the biblical site of Mount Sinai—supposedly the place where God reached down to Earth and handed Moses the Ten Commandments.

Why trek through the Egyptian desert in the middle of the summer? Well, we were in our late teens and had gone in search of a religious experience.

Now one piece of advice if you're going to hike the holiest mountain on Earth in the middle of the summer. Don't eat pigeon in a cheap restaurant in Cairo the day before you embark on the adventure. Why not, you ask? Two words: explosive diarrhea. Exactly what I was suffering with as I hiked up this mystical mountain.

As if that wasn't bad enough, it was also unbearably hot and I was dehydrating fast. (We foolishly began our hike in the early morning, thus climbed as it got progressively hotter.)

Despite my diarrhea and dehydration, I persisted, though I truly thought I was going to collapse at any moment. I even remember thinking that if you're gonna go, what a legendary way to die: while hiking the holiest mountain in the world. After hours I began to hallucinate colors and shapes just as we reached the peak of the mountain. If Moses saw a burning bush, I was suffering from a burning butt.

Despite the conditions being ripe for a life-altering religious experience, nothing really happened to me at the top of the mountain. Try as I might, no visions appeared and God didn't send me any messages.

Once back in Israel I also tried to have this type of religious awakening in Jerusalem. I went to the Western Wall, the Church of the Holy Sepulchre, and the Dome of the Rock, always in hopes of having some profound existential moment. Again, this life-affirming moment remained elusive.

Despite growing up around religious stories, from Hebrew school to holidays, I never was able to fully understand the need for biblical stories. Amazingly, visiting the most ancient holy sites didn't do the trick, but spending a year with Jordan did just that.

He has convinced me that societies run better when they operate under a belief system that stems from timeless, age-old biblical truths.

This doesn't mean he wants people to be religious, per se—in fact, I've never once heard him say this. He simply wants people to take their moral codes from an objective reality outside of themselves.

Initially, I wasn't convinced by this. Like Steven Pinker and Sam Harris, I leaned toward the idea that human beings can conceive similar ideas without the need for religious aspect. Old stories were just that—old stories—and surely they could be replaced with newer, better ones that were more relevant to our modern world. If we as a species had progressed, then surely our stories had to progress along with us.

Jordan and Sam Harris took part in several debates in front of thousands on this very topic right in the middle of our 12 Rules tour.

Could we humans leave it to our intellect alone to come up

with a timeless moral code, as Sam would argue, or do we need something else, something rooted in the divine outside ourselves, to safeguard our freedoms?

While my default position on this was with Sam, I gradually found Jordan's argument to be more coherent.

As we have progressed in terms of freedoms, rights, and tolerance, we have regressed in defense of what got us here in the first place. Postmodernism, now the main school of thought at so many of our academic institutions, has rejected objective truth in exchange for subjective feelings.

Yes, enlightenment values are objectively good, but that's not enough. The ideas of reason, individual liberty, and a representative government have to come from somewhere beyond just the human mind. For if they come from us, then they can be taken away by us. They must be built upon a foundation that is unchangeable and unalterable by the whims of man.

So while enlightenment values come from man, and work in an ideal world when everything's going smoothly, they alone can't withstand man's eternal battles over freedom versus authoritarianism.

Speaking as a person who isn't particularly religious, this is a strange place for me to argue from, but it is one I see no way around. Throughout history, every socialist or communist state tried to replace God with government. Lots of people have to die in order to get us to that Shangri-la . . . one, of course, that never comes.

I know, I know—religions have also caused death and destruction. And in no way am I defending those atrocities. What I am saying, however, is that the concepts expressed throughout the eternal stories that religion has brought us have proved fundamental to our beliefs and freedoms even if we don't want them to be.

Do you believe the little guy can beat the big guy? Well, David beat Goliath. It is an eternal belief that generations share. This idea—that humans can accomplish anything against the odds—is exactly what distinguishes us as human in the first place.

Plus, in the face of growing authoritarianism and tyranny, these eternal truths have also offered us mechanisms to become better versions of ourselves.

Most religions provide us with a redemption narrative. You can go to confession or attend mikvah and cleanse yourself. But today's leftism, which is just another form of collectivism that has arisen over the ages, makes you born guilty, especially if you are a white Christian male—this is the left's version of original sin. There's no redemption, ever. Only eternal damnation. Bow forever or be excommunicated.

All this being said, of course individuals can be godless and still be good. *Some of my best friends are atheists!*

This isn't about the individual level though; this is about how humanity can flourish over time and withstand the human forces that would see us enslave, impoverish, and enforce our own values over someone else's.

The only antidote for that is a truth outside of us. A moral code as a light in the darkness. I see no way around it, as much as my enlightenment brain would like to. The eternal truths told for thousands of years through biblical stories are the rudder that keeps us moving forward during the storm. And have no doubt, a storm is a-comin'.

This is why Jordan's biblical lectures have been viewed millions of times by people all over the world. Or why *The Right Side of History*, which explains the connection of Judeo-Christian values from Jerusalem to Athens, has resonated with so many the way it has.

So while my personal religious awakening remains a work in progress, it is actually my intellect that has led me to believe in something beyond me.

Perhaps I did get my religious experience, after all . . .

EMBRACE PARENTHOOD

No, I'm not talking about the Steve Martin movie from 1989, *Parenthood*. (Though between peak Steve Martin, a young Keanu Reeves, and the vibrator scene with Dianne Wiest, it's absolutely worth the $3.99 rental.)

I'm talking about the importance of actually having children.

This might just be the single greatest lesson I learned while traveling with Jordan, which I appreciate isn't very rock n roll.

While many people return from touring with drug problems and cirrhosis of the liver, perhaps even a sexually transmitted disease or two, I came back home with an abstract wisdom about fatherhood.

This explains why our tour manager, John, always joked we were the lamest tour he'd ever been involved with. No trashed hotel rooms, no hookers, and no drugs. The biggest scandal we had the entire time was when I accidentally said, "It's great to be here in Edmonton!" when in fact we were in Toronto. Awkward.

Somehow though, along the way of this tour, I had a profound personal insight into something that I had been avoiding for all of my adult life.

I never really wanted children. This was my firmly held view from a young age that persisted throughout my adult life, even after meeting my husband in 2009.

As someone who was in the closet for many years, I never envisioned a future for myself, really. Not only that, but gay marriage wasn't even legal until I was in my late thirties. Even putting aside my personal feelings about having kids, if I couldn't get married first, then it didn't even seem like a realistic thing to think about. For my husband, David, this was very different. He's twelve years younger than I, came out much earlier, and always wanted a family of his own. He often tells me he grew up knowing that he was gay and wanting a family and kids. These were all far-off, almost totally unrealistic ideas for me as a child of the 80s. There was just no proof any of it could happen or was even on the horizon.

As gay marriage passed and our lives stabilized together, the discussion about kids would pop up now and again. (Always spurred on by David, and hastily shut down by me.)

It wasn't as if Mother Nature was on our side. Although straight people can become parents without even trying, gay couples need to plan conception like a surgical operation, involving doctors, nurses, test tubes, and surrogates.

Why put ourselves through that stress when we could indulge a lifetime of impulsive pleasures instead? These were the cards we were handed, and maybe there's some real freedom in that. Maybe straight people spread the genes and gay people spread the memes.

After all, my gay friends often seem happier than my straight friends, and they almost always look a lot better. This was my perspective right up until the beginning of the tour, which is when everything began to change.

Night after night, I'd hear Jordan say that the overwhelming majority of people need the timeless experience of parenthood in order to live authentic, fully realized lives. Sure, a minority of people can get a similar fulfillment through friendships, careers, and intellectual pursuits, but not many. These people are an incredibly small fraction of the population.

Everybody else is kidding themselves, distracting themselves, or ultimately regretful that they've missed the boat.

This notion struck a chord with me one night. Was my life as fulfilled as I thought it was? Was the show, the tour, my dog, or even my marriage really enough?

Could I be the exception to the rule? And even if I was, what kind of person would I be if my wishes overrode the wishes of the person I chose to spend the rest of my life with?

That's when I knew I'd been looking at it all wrong. And perhaps it's connected to the lesson about biblical stories that was just discussed in the previous section. Life isn't just about happiness, it is also about meaning and purpose. Seeing Jordan inspire so many people to find their meaning and purpose suddenly shifted what I felt mine was as well.

Before this realization, I'd put so much energy into my career, and it defined me for so long, that I was worried I might lose it—perhaps even myself—by becoming a father.

As the tour went on, and I heard this message in a new way each night, the rubber eventually hit the proverbial road. It was time.

Several months later, toward the end of the tour, Jordan and I were sitting at dinner in a local steakhouse in Perth, Australia. I'd never shared it with anyone before, but told Jordan and his wife, Tammy, that David and I had finally begun the surrogacy process.

They were literally the first people I told, which was a conception in and of itself, and they both lit up with pure joy. (This reaction from Jordan also affirmed another one of his 12 Rules, Rule 3: "Make friends with people who want the best for you."

Jordan told me he knew I'd make a great father and that he could see my life getting richer from that moment forward. I'm guessing he's probably right.

I'll let you know for sure as the kid enters its teenage years . . .

LAUGH

So as you can see, I learned some pretty valuable lessons from Jordan Peterson, but I also think that I managed to teach him a couple of things too.

Specifically, the value of humor.

One night in the middle of the tour, I did my own ninety-minute stand-up show at Wisecrackers Comedy Club in Salt Lake City, Utah. I did a bunch of these one-off solo gigs on nights when we would get to town a day early. Usually, I'd do about an hour of stand-up and then bring on a guest direct from the Intellectual Dark Web for a chat and audience Q and A. We did this about a dozen times with Eric and Bret Weinstein, Christina Hoff Sommers, Michael Shermer, and others.

I had circled one date in Salt Lake specifically though because I was going to bring Jordan onto the stage as my guest, and it would be the first time he got to see me as a comic outside of the confines of the warm-up and Q and A guy. I really wanted to crush it that night because I wanted Jordan to see me fully doing my thing.

What started as a need for approval permanently changed the dynamic of our relationship.

The crowd was electric all night long, and that electricity went nuclear when I brought my surprise guest onstage. We told some stories, cracked some jokes, I think Jordan even cursed a couple times, and everyone exploded out of their seats into a standing ovation when it was over.

But in my opinion, the best outcome was that Jordan himself found a new appreciation not only for me but also for the power of comedy. Sure, he already knew it intellectually and on a personal level (he takes great pleasure from the fact he introduced his children to *The Simpsons* sitcom and to the Jim Carrey comedy *The Mask*), but I could see how, after this show, he incorporated more comedy into his lectures.

A short while after that, I had preplanned family commitments in New York City and couldn't be part of our show, so Jordan went onstage alone—without any warm-up.

That evening, he sent me a message that contained the best compliment of my career to date: "I much prefer the shows with you," he said.

"They're lighter and more fun. They work much better. See you soon."

Wow. I'd moved somebody I admired through the power of funny. That's as good as it gets for somebody like me.

As time went on I saw a slight change in how he performed. He was more willing to make the occasional joke or flash a wry smile while talking about the unremitting tragedy of human life. Ironically, often his funniest moments were unintentionally hilarious, like when citing a study about rats doing cocaine. The crowd would laugh at the mere premise and then I'd see him ad-lib a couple more lines around it.

One night I told him that within a couple short months he could become a legendary comedian if he wanted to. He was already telling the truth, now he just needed a few more jokes to build out the set.

Jordan never became a comic, but his wisdom was no doubt enhanced by his use of humor in his lectures. And although I still think he could be a brilliant comic one day, I know it's not in his future because he always commits the biggest comedy no-no . . . when you're getting a big laugh you pause and milk it for as long as possible. But Jordan, with so much more to say and with such limited time, would usually just plow through the laugh as if it didn't happen. Our tour manager, John, a former comic, and I would constantly watch Jordan talk through the laughs in alternating bewilderment and awe.

So although Jordan may not be a perfect stand-up comic, his use of comedy is key. As the free speech battle continues—he illustrates that comedy can be our most effective weapon.

Not only does comedy disarm your audience by giving them room to laugh at themselves, but it also gives you much-needed room to be a truth-teller. Your motive is mirth, not malice. You can sneak the most important things into the midst of all the laughter. This is the tightrope that all truly great comics must walk.

Comedians are like canaries in the coal mine of life, which is precisely why authoritarians of the past and present were, and still are, so intent on silencing them.

From banning gay jokes on *Family Guy* to trying to boot Apu from *The Simpsons*, or making comedians like Chris Rock feel unwelcome on college campuses, progressives are now censoring life's truth-tellers.

So if you want to function efficiently in our increasingly polarizing society, I urge you to find those laughs whenever and wherever possible. Laugh at both the state of the world and at ourselves. In doing so, it allows us to acknowledge our flaws while also transcending them.

This is why I'd often use our Q and A sessions to ask Jordan if he'd be willing to voice Kermit the Frog in the next Muppet movie. Or whether he wears boxers or briefs. Often after he'd answer a question in a particularly long-winded way, and I'd say, "So what you're saying is . . . ," which was a callback to his infamous interview with Cathy Newman of Channel 4 News in the United Kingdom.

Everyone in the audience knew exactly what I was doing and you could feel the wave of laughter wash over the crowd. We were all in this thing together.

These moments would allow Jordan to laugh at himself and not take himself too seriously. No matter what ridiculous question I would ask, he would take it in stride. These brief moments between serious questions about suicide, gender pronouns, and the fate of Western civilization allowed the audience to revel in the absurd while also dealing with deeply difficult issues.

As Oscar Wilde once said, "If you want to tell somebody the truth you'd better make it funny otherwise they'll kill you."

YOU TOO CAN CHANGE THE WORLD

People often think of Jordan as a Jesus-like figure, but he's just as human as you or me.

Yes, it's true. The man who has transformed the world through incredible amounts of video views and millions of books sold is just a regular guy from the frigid Northern Alberta tundra.

What distinguishes Jordan isn't his incredible academic résumé, his years in clinical practice, or the impressive research he's conducted.

What distinguishes Jordan from the rest of us is that he actually went out there and changed the world. First, he cleaned his room (Rule 6), then he moved on to cleaning the world.

I know this because I saw it firsthand. It wasn't just that Jordan dressed better for the tour, but he actually became more intellectually rigorous as it went on. I saw him stretch the limits of what he could truthfully say each and every night. He stood up to every smear piece and lie the media threw at him. He bravely walked into the fire when most people would've run the other way. Actually, I should note that he would often say that he didn't enjoy the combative nature of his relationship with the media, because he isn't particularly interested in conflict (he would also be sure to note that there were plenty of fair and honest pieces written about him). But he passionately stood up for himself when attacked and that made other people do the same for him . . . and ultimately for themselves.

There are countless personal stories about people who have gone from chaos to order by incorporating Jordan's rules into their lives. Show after show I could see the magic happen. It wasn't smoke and mirrors—it was real, tangible, and transformational change, which never ceased to amaze me.

One evening in Manchester, England, a father and son approached us in tears outside the theater. They'd been estranged for twelve years, yet randomly ran into each other in the audience that evening. These were not tears of sadness though, but joy. Whatever had torn them apart over a decade earlier, Jordan had given them the road map to come back together. They cleaned their houses, ended their personal chaos separately, and then, almost by divine intervention, ended up in the same theater only to find each other once again. The chaos had come to a close.

Another time we met a sharply dressed young man at the Copenhagen Airport in Denmark. He'd been waiting there for hours on the off chance he could present Jordan with an essay he'd written about how he'd been positively affected by 12 Rules for Life.

He told us that he'd waited at the exit all day, just in the hope that Jordan was flying in the day of the show. It was a lark, and it worked. Though we were in a bit of a rush to get to the hotel before the show, Jordan stopped, chatted with the man for a few minutes, and gladly took the essay, which he read while in the car en route to the hotel.

I don't know what was in the essay, but I saw Jordan slowly nodding along as he read it during the drive.

Then there was the time we'd boarded a plane to travel from Stockholm to Helsinki for another show. As the airport staff began to close the doors of the plane, a young man in charge of the jet bridge rushed on to thank Jordan for changing his life.

He emotionally explained that his relationships and career had improved immeasurably as a result of Jordan's intervention. Tears of joy were welling up in his eyes.

"I got this job because of you," he said.

These are just a small sampling of the instances in which I saw firsthand how Jordan helped other people by helping himself first. These people would often talk about how their lives being in order not only helped them at work but also at home, in their relationships, and even physically. In many cases, perhaps even all of them, they would then pass this transformational experience on to others, who hopefully did the same.

The good news is that you can do this too. Fix yourself before you fix the world. Not the other way around. Speak your truth and stand strong in the face of criticism just as Jordan has. You can change your reality by doing this. Trust me, I know.

My own life was enriched and bettered by being on that 12 Rules tour for a year and a half. The messages that I heard over and over seeped into me and made me a better person. Not a perfect person, but someone who constantly tries to better himself.

As I did this, I saw the results manifest in my own life: our shows got better night after night, my relationships improved, I evolved on personal issues I was stuck on (that whole father thing) as well as spiritually, and—as a nice bonus—even made a few more bucks along the way.

It sounds too good to be true, but it's not. You can actually alter the nature of reality by living your truth and applying it to the world. If you lie, your lies will spread and reality will unfurl into chaos. But if you speak truth and instill order, you have no idea of the goodness you can create.

And here's the best part: there's never been a better time to do this.

A hundred years ago your thoughts wouldn't have spread very far. You might've been able to have influence among your immediate family or a couple of people in your local town, but unless you were a successful writer, that would've been about it.

If you sent a letter it would've taken days to arrive—if it got there at all.

Now, you can be naked on the toilet at 3:00 a.m. and create a meme that goes viral, reaches millions of people, and makes them think.

You've never had such incredible power and reach. We have no idea how that awesome power has changed the world already and will continue to do so. So how are you going to use that power? What do you want to put out into the universe?

Begin your adventure now and you will be amazed at how you can change your world. But, before you start, don't forget to clean your room.

10

Move On with Your Life

SEVERAL YEARS AGO, a palliative care nurse hit the headlines when she revealed the most common regrets among her dying patients.

Bronnie Ware, from Australia, spent countless hours in hospice wards where she gleaned wisdom from the terminally ill and their unique perspective on life.

Her insight first appeared in a viral blog post and later became the premise of her bestselling book, *The Top Five Regrets of the Dying*.

In it, almost everyone she spoke to said the exact same thing: they wished they'd spent more time off-duty with family and friends, rather than working long hours, fighting the tide, and fretting over pointless nonsense that drained them of energy, perspective, and joy.

Specifically, they said:

I wish I'd had the courage to live a life true to myself, not
the life others expected of me
I wish I hadn't worked so hard

I wish I'd had the courage to express my feelings

I wish I had stayed in touch with my friends

I wish that I had let myself be happier

Although Ware's findings were anecdotal, a study by Cornell University and The New School for Social Research in 2018 reinforced them. Their analysis used six separate tests to conclude that "people are more likely to regret not being all they *could* have been, more than all they *should* have been."

Essentially, what these people are saying is that they wished they'd lived their lives unapologetically. Above all else, that is what I hope this book gives you permission to do. I want to empower you not only to speak your mind when it comes to politics, but also to live the life you actually want to live, unfettered by the trends of the moment.

My deepest hope is that this book elevates you, the individual, to think for yourself and truly be free.

Sounds obvious, right? Maybe even a no-brainer. Except barely anyone is actually doing it. Most people are so engrossed in the drama of the moment—both personal and political—that they cannot see how good they actually have it.

In a time when the standard of living has never been higher, we are acting like the world is coming to an end. Whether you're a baby boomer addicted to watching cable news, a millennial hooked on Twitter conflict, or a zoomer who comes home from school fearing the end of the world because of climate change, I'm here to tell you to cool your jets.

Psychologists have a word for this behavior: *catastrophizing*. When we catastrophize, we engage in an irrational thought process that leads us to believe something is far worse than it actually is.

Take, for example, the remarks of sixteen-year-old climate activist Greta Thunberg, which she delivered angry and teary-eyed at the 2019 Climate Action Summit:

"You have stolen my dreams and childhood with your empty words. . . . People are suffering. People are dying," she pontificated.

"Entire ecosystems are collapsing. We are in the beginning of a mass extinction, and all you can talk about is money and fairy-tales about economic growth. How dare you."

Potential exploitation of a clinically depressed teenager aside, her catastrophizing only causes unnecessary moral alarm among people who, realistically, have no plans to dedicate themselves to the global warming "crisis."

Greta's shtick is all smoke and mirrors, but it's getting a lot of people worked up, biasing them against their future plans, like having children, for fear that the Earth will be destroyed.

Catastrophizing isn't a partisan problem—it's a global one. We're all guilty of making the exact same mistakes every single day of our lives: focusing way too much on petty nonsense while letting personal relationships, happiness, and inner peace slide.

Our tendency to do this to ourselves is nothing new. Human beings have always allowed their personal priorities to fall by the wayside as they juggled different tasks to advance big goals. However, although we have a long history of being distracted by things that eventually benefit us, from hunting to feed our cave-dwelling family all the way to working long office hours to afford the down payment on a first house, we now seem to be preoccupied with problems that sap our energy and have no long-term reward.

If there is a crisis that needs to be addressed, it's our culture of crisis itself—or what we have come to call a culture war. You know what I'm talking about: the bizarre fashion of being all-consumed by the big, impersonal stuff that divides us while overlooking all the little things that make us happy, centered, connected people.

Clearly, we've learned nothing from the mass hysterias throughout history, such as the Salem Witch trials of 1692, The Great Fear of 1789, or *The War of The Worlds* radio broadcast in 1938. Here we are, still allowing ourselves to be held in the grip of group agitation, every single day of the week. Even our favorite holidays aren't off-limits.

Only recently John Legend and Kelly Clarkson marked Christmas by reworking the festive classic "Baby, It's Cold Outside" to include feminist lyrics about consensual sex in a post-MeToo era. For the record, I stand with Dean Martin, now and always.

Then there's the staff at *Newsweek*, who published a guide to having a "woke Thanksgiving." Yes, really.

Their advice ranged from tackling climate change by minimizing food waste to making Donald Trump the main topic of conversation at the dinner table (as well as the horrors of the Republican tax cuts). They also suggested boycotting the great Thanksgiving tradition of American football by tackling "the issue of head trauma among current and former NFL players."

Ironically, you can probably get head trauma by reading such drivel.

These are tragic examples of a very modern affliction. One that grinds people down into the living embodiment of Debbie Downer from *Saturday Night Live*—a show that has also become a victim of its own messiah complex. What was once smart, irreverent, and bitingly funny sketch comedy is now angry, resentful, and brittle.

Clearly, people are losing their minds and their sense of humor, but more than just our sanity is at stake in the culture war. So is our freedom.

When we fail to live a life outside politics, we become a slave to it. While it's certainly important to be aware of all the issues I've discussed here, it's way more important to live a well-rounded, fully-realized life that's regularly removed from all the drama.

In order to do this, we must learn to distinguish between being politically engaged and politically obsessed.

As Sonny Bunch wrote in *The Washington Free Beacon*:

> There isn't anything wrong with living a political life. Politics is important; political decisions have consequences; and passionately arguing for your preferred political outcomes is nothing to be ashamed of. [But] a politicized life is a different beast, however. It treats politics as a zero-sum game or a form of total warfare in which the other side must be obliterated.
>
> It alters every aspect of your being: where you shop; what you watch on TV; what sort of music you listen to; who you associate with. If you're not with the politicized being, you're against him—and if you're against him, he is well within his rights to ruin you personally and economically. You, the political other, are a leper to be shunned.

This sentiment was later echoed by Karl Salzmann in the *National Review*:

> Politics are at best a necessary evil. They exist not as an end in themselves but as a means of strengthening and uniting the civic ties that bind us as a people and a nation.

If we choose to center our lives completely on politics, then we forget why we have them in the first place. We cannot love policy-prescriptions, but we can love people, and we ought to realize that when we're tempted to politicize every aspect of our society—from pageants to sports to film and television to our interactions with others.

It reminds me of what the late, great Christopher Hitchens once said when he described alcohol as being "a better slave than a master." To some extent, the same thing applies here with the political culture war. Sensible indulgence is fine (it can often be a ton of fun), but bingeing on it from the moment you wake up is not.

When this happens, it's time to press the reset button and reclaim control.

Unfortunately, there's never been a trickier time to try to break this cycle. Why? Because it's facilitated by a new, powerful distraction that previous generations never had to deal with—one that's literally designed to keep us trapped in a constant state of conflict, suspense, and panic: social technology.

According to Aza Raskin, the smartphone's infinite scroll feature (which allows us to swipe down continuously without clicking) was deliberately built to be habit-forming. He should know. He's the engineer who created it.

"Behind every screen on your phone, there are literally a thousand engineers that have worked on this thing to try to make it maximally addicting," he told the BBC's investigative journalism show *Panorama*. "You have a business model designed to engage you and get you to basically suck as much time out of your life as possible and then selling that attention to advertisers."

If that sounds about right, it's probably because it is. And, like so many others, I know this from personal experience.

Back in December 2008, when I first joined Twitter (ironically on Christmas day), I did so out of sheer curiosity. The iPhone was still new and just the act of downloading an app seemed like something cool. Then I quickly found myself hooked on all the craziness, like a junkie who'd just gotten a new drug.

The constant interaction seemed fresh and exciting. Getting a "mic drop" moment provided a weird sense of victory, while "owning" somebody over a particular issue was equally satisfying.

Of course, like any addiction, I soon couldn't get enough of my new vice. I found myself chasing the next dopamine-laced thrill. This involved scrolling through mindless drivel for hours and hours, despite the fact that my poor brain wasn't registering half of the words I read.

I'd even wake up during the night to check my phone, then double-check it again just in case I'd missed anything. (Guess what, I hadn't.)

Before long, I began to feel stressed by this compulsion and other things I couldn't possibly control, such as a stranger's opinion of me or whether I got the last word in a Twitter spat.

I would also become embroiled in pointless arguments with random strangers, even though I knew it wasn't good for me. Every fight felt like the most important thing in the world—until the next one. And the next one. And the next one . . .

It came at the expense of my attention span, my ability to concentrate, and even my manners at the table. I'd be out with friends or hosting a dinner party, selfishly checking my messages in the middle of a conversation.

I was seeking out the conflict and getting a kick out of it. Political drama and confrontation became my new normal, making everyday conversations seem boring—even though they were about actual things happening in my real life.

As a result, I started to develop a one-track mind. French poet Alain de Lille once said that all roads lead to Rome. But in my newly addled brain, all roads led me back to me and my online ego. I couldn't switch off.

This, folks, is what it looks like when perspective diminishes in real time. I was becoming somebody I didn't particularly recognize or like.

So, at this point, I decided to detox my life and went cold turkey by locking my smartphone in a safe for a month. It wasn't exactly checking into the Betty Ford clinic, but it worked.

For the first few days I actually got physical withdrawal symptoms from all the adrenaline; I was jittery and fidgety. Then, I developed weird reflexes, which made me reach for my device every time I heard somebody else's message alert. I developed a serious case of FOMO, the notorious "fear of missing out."

Thankfully, after a short while, things improved. I began to sleep better, and old songs would randomly pop into my head as the available space in my brain got freed up. I also became less anxious and more present in my daily life.

According to the people around me, including my mother-in-law, the results were noticeable—I'd officially got my old, "pre-phone" self back. And it felt good.

To this day I still take weekends off the grid and try to have entire days without any electronic gadgets.

Obviously, I'm not saying that technology is all bad. My career and life have clearly been transformed by YouTube and that whole universe, but there certainly seems to be a weird link between today's hyperpartisan divisions and our mass, 24-7 connectivity.

But smartphones, iPads, and laptops are not the issue. Rather, it's the fact that they're all lightning rods to the heart of the problem.

So it's not enough to simply power down your devices. You also need to silence the nagging voice in your head—the one that points out every real or imagined political prompt and tells you to react.

Back in the 1940s, British prime minister Winston Churchill described his clinical depression as a black dog—a sinister companion on life's journey. One that followed him around to every occasion and cast a long shadow over his joy. Whenever he tried to outrun it, or hide from it, it would inevitably find him and pounce.

Many years later in 2009, author Sally Brampton penned a self-help book about her own depression called *Shoot the Damn Dog*.

This instruction is precisely what I want you to do with the canine that's living in your brain. You know, the one that sniffs out every little thing for a political bone, then barks like crazy.

It may sound drastic, but this is crucial for your own well-being.

Otherwise, it's a guarantee that you are wasting your time and energy, which—as I pointed out at the beginning of this chapter—are the only things you'll wish you had not squandered when the Grim Reaper comes calling. And he will.

So, in keeping with all the other guidance I've offered in these pages, here are some other tips for enjoying a balanced life in this crazy world:

- No TV in the bedroom. This sacred space should be for sleeping or having sex. Ideally, sleeping after sex, but you get the idea. Not having a TV allows you to focus your attention on the bed itself, which, as the name suggests, is what this space is all about.
- Similarly, keep your phone in another room overnight. Your day shouldn't start and end with staring into that little black mirror. It's virtually impossible to achieve true intimacy with your partner or get a decent night's sleep when you're thinking about the messages waiting for you on your nightstand.
- Have cutoff times for social media and news. At some point in the evening, stop looking at either. Given the twenty-four-hour media cycle, you need to be strict in enforcing this. Otherwise, your time will be taken by people who (A) don't respect it and (B) don't deserve it. Setting these boundaries will help separate your real world from the never-ending digital world. Let reality have the last word, every single day.
- When you're out to dinner with a group of friends, play a game where everyone stacks their phone in the middle of the table. The first to cave and retrieve their device must pay the check. This keeps you present and focused in the moment, which I'm guessing is why you're there in the first place.
- Twice each year, take a one-week break from social media. I recommend the last week of the summer and the final

week of the year—this will recharge your batteries at convenient times and restore your perspective. Then slowly reintroduce yourself to it all with fresh eyes. (If you're feeling really adventurous, join me once a year for the month of August, when I shut off all my devices and stop reading the news entirely.)

- In general, be more discerning in your use of Facebook. It's a hotbed of grievance-stoking and self-indulgence that has limited benefits for most people, so feel free to unfollow or mute those who make your experience miserable. This encourages you to stay focused on your own life, rather than the inconsequential happenings of others. In fact, use this approach with all of your online activity. Ration how much of your life you're willing to sacrifice online. Naturally, I want the internet to be as free and open as possible, but the way we consume it should be conservative in the true sense—as in literally conserving something worth saving. In this instance, your happiness and your sanity.

- Get in contact with old friends. If you have pre-internet pals, revive your relationships with them. It's more important than you might think. It will remind you of who you were before this madness happened. It rekindles an element of innocence in your life, which is hard to find in an era of mass cynicism.

- Introduce yourself to your neighbors. Immediate, face-to-face interaction with real people who live on your street helps to cultivate a sense of community. It's a daily reminder that we have more in common than apart, even if you live next door to the crazy cat lady.

- Appreciate your family. There's a twisted narrative out there that it's fashionable to belittle your parents and your relatives, but this is who you are and where you come from. Maintaining good bonds with your loved ones is the starting point for how you treat the rest of the world. It's a master class in acceptance. That's where you hone your tolerance skills before applying them to the wider world. It's a constant tutorial in compromise, so dip in regularly and top up the gas in your tank. This makes you a better person. Especially if you can love someone you got stuck with just because of your genes.

- Host a holiday in your home. Tradition matters. You can start new traditions or retain old ones, but the idea is that it brings us all back to the center to recalibrate. It reminds us of what's important in life. Without it, we risk losing our priorities, which as I've already noted is a no-no.

- Sense of humor. Get one! As much as you have a duty to protect yourself from becoming perma-political and joyless, you've also got a responsibility not to ruin everybody else's fun, too. Nobody wants to hang out with somebody who's forever bitching and being a buzzkill. It's exhausting. So allow yourself to laugh, even if the joke isn't politically correct.

- Practice the art of being diplomatic. Just because we can voice our opinion on every little thing doesn't mean we should. Sometimes, tuning out is just as important as tuning in. This applies to us all, including me.

There's a curious irony to this last chapter, considering I've written something that sounds the alarm about our current state of affairs.

Yes, free speech is under attack, and people are forgetting what it means to truly be free. But guess what: the only way to combat this crisis is to get on with our lives as if there isn't one—speaking our minds without self-censoring, living our values without apology, and loving who we damn well please.

Yes, we can speak up in favor of freedom, but our greater obligation is choosing to actually live it, every single day.

If you do this, your existence will reverberate in ways you can't imagine. That's exactly what happened to me, just a regular guy from Long Island, and it all started by saying what I think.

So, while I'm very flattered that you've chosen to read this book, I also want you to finish it, close the back cover, and put it away, both literally and metaphorically.

Thinking for yourself is all you need in an age of unreason.

ACKNOWLEDGMENTS

First, I must thank the sweet girl lying by my feet as I write this, Emma. At fifteen and a half years old, I don't know if she'll make it to the release date of the book, but she's been my constant companion during this whole journey.

Second, I must thank my husband, David, for a million reasons, including that he'll love that I thanked Emma first. Since we met on my birthday in 2009, my life has forever changed for the better. Every bit of my success and happiness is because of his relentless passion, curiosity, and love for life.

Of course, none of this would've been possible without my parents, Carol and Ira, who taught me that nothing in the world is more important than family.

My brother, Jonathan, and my sister, Talia, have become true friends. Both of you are incredible siblings, as well as spouses and parents, and my admiration for you increases constantly.

And my extended family, who taught me how to argue without hating and to get together for the important moments no matter what.

To Cip and Ari for being my videogame/sports/intellectual sparring partners for almost forty years.

My team at *The Rubin Report*, who make sure I sit up in my chair and keep me on schedule and on point. (Special shout-out to Helen for making sure I never get lost, which is a job unto itself.)

Alexis for making me look awake when I'm tired, and Jess for making my hair look full, even when it was literally falling out of my head. And Amiria, who quit nearly fifteen different jobs to help us build the *Rubin Report*.

To Ari Levin and Justin Edbrooke at CAA, who saw me perform only once before we signed together, and to Anthony Mattero, who got this book deal without my even asking.

My other Helen, Helen Healey, my editor at Penguin, who was an absolute pro throughout the writing process and always found a way to push me in the right direction, even when I didn't know it.

Adrian Zackheim, my publisher at Penguin, as well as my book publicists Margot Stamas, Jamie Lescht, and Mary Kate Skehan.

Peter Lloyd, who helped me more than anyone else to work through and clarify the ideas presented in this book. A total professional, a great thinker, and a good man.

Larry King for being the greatest interviewer ever, a mentor, and a bonus grandfather.

Clyde Drexler for showing me if you play hard enough and long enough, you can win a championship.

Dorothy Zbornak, a substitute teacher from Brooklyn, who lived in Miami with her mother and two best friends and was one of my first classical liberal influences.

And most importantly, to you, the people who show me love and appreciation every day just for saying what I think. I hope I've given back to you just a fraction of what you've given me. Thank you. Thank you. Thank you.

NOTES

CHAPTER 2: EMBRACE YOUR WAKE-UP CALL

25 **"teenagers across the globe":** Jeff Sossamon, "Countries with Greater Gender Equality Have Lower Percentage of Female STEM Graduates, MU Study Finds," University of Missouri News Bureau, February 14, 2018, https://munewsarchives.missouri.edu /news-releases/2018/0214-countries-with-greater-gender-equality-have-lower -percentage-of-female-stem-graduates-mu-study-finds/.

CHAPTER 3: THINK FREELY OR DIE

47 **canceled president of Planned Parenthood:** "Dr. Leana Wen to Serve as President of Planned Parenthood." Press release. September 12, 2018. www.planned parenthood.org/about-us/newsroom/press-releases/planned-parenthood -announcement.

56 **gun-related homicides increased:** Maya Rhodan, "Gun-Related Deaths in America Keep Going Up," *Time*, November 6, 2017. https://time.com/5011599/gun-deaths -rate-america-cdc-data/.

61 **U.S. Transgender Survey from 2015:** Sandy E. James, Jody L. Herman, Susan Rankin, Mara Keisling, Lisa Mottet, and Ma'ayan Anafi, *The Report of the 2015 U.S. Transgender Survey*, National Center for Transgender Equality, December 2016, www.transequality.org/sites/default/files/docs/USTS-Full-Report-FINAL .PDF.

65 **doesn't institute it at his own company:** Robert Bellafiore, *Summary of the Latest Federal Income Tax Data, 2018 Update*, Tax Foundation, November 13, 2018, https:// taxfoundation.org/summary-latest-federal-income-tax-data-2018-update/.

66 **the world's largest economy:** Bill Chappell, "U.S. National Debt Hits Record $22 Trillion," NPR, February 13, 2019, www.npr.org/2019/02/13/694199256/u-s -national-debt-hits-22-trillion-a-new-record-thats-predicted-to-fall?t=1572892 870713.

CHAPTER 4: DON'T WORRY, YOU'RE NOT A NAZI

75 **"biggest illusionist associated":** Philipp Oehmke, "The Alt-Right Movement Behind Trump's Presidency," *Der Spiegel*, July 14, 2017, www.spiegel.de/international/world /the-alt-right-movement-behind-trump-s-presidency-a-1155901-2.html.

CHAPTER 5: CHECK YOUR FACTS, NOT YOUR PRIVILEGE

92 **According to talkpoverty.org:** Katharine Gallagher Robbins, "The Media Narrative Around Families Is Racist and Homophobic. It Needs to Stop," TalkPoverty, June 23, 2017, https://talkpoverty.org/2017/06/23/media-narrative-around-families-racist -homophobic-needs-stop/.

98 **National Opinion Research Center:** *The Associated Press–NORC Center for Public Affairs Research and General Social Survey*, Changing Attitudes about Racial Inequality, March 2019, www.apnorc.org/PDFs/GSS%202018/APNORC_GSS_race_relations_report _2019.pdf.

98 **Harvard University's Tessa Charlesworth:** Tessa E. S. Charlesworth and Mahzarin R. Banaji, "Patterns of Implicit and Explicit Attitudes: I. Long-Term Change and Stability from 2007 to 2016," *Psychological Science* 30, no. 4 (January 2019): 174–92, https://journals.sagepub.com/doi/10.1177/0956797618813087.

100 **"the better chance we have":** National Center for Children in Poverty, *Poverty by the Numbers*, November 20, 2007, www.nccp.org/media/releases/release_34.html.

100 **Women dominate universities:** Will Martin, "The 19 Countries with the Highest Ratio of Women to Men in Higher Education," *The Independent (London)*, November 22, 2015, www.independent.co.uk/news/education/education-news/the-19-countries-with -the-highest-ratio-of-women-to-men-in-higher-education-a6743976.html.

101 **women made up more:** U.S. Department of Education, National Center for Education Statistics, Higher Education General Information Survey, "Fall Enrollment in Colleges and Universities." Total undergraduate fall enrollment in degree-granting postsecondary institutions, by attendance status, sex of student, and control and level of institution: Selected years, 1970 through 2026, February 2017, table 303.70, https://nces.ed.gov/programs/digest/d16/tables/dt16_303.70.asp.

101 **women were 36 percent more likely:** Universities and College Admissions Service, "Rise in Rate of 18 Year Olds Applying for UK Higher Education," February 5, 2018, www.ucas.com/corporate/news-and-key-documents/news/rise-rate-18-year-olds -applying-uk-higher-education.

101 **80 percent of murder victims:** United Nations Office on Drugs and Crime, *World Drug Report 2013*, May 2013, www.unodc.org/unodc/secured/wdr/wdr2013/World _Drug_Report_2013.pdf.

101 **harassed for their political views:** Maeve Duggan, *Online Harassment 2017*, Pew Research Center, July 11, 2017, www.pewresearch.org/internet/2017/07/11/online -harassment-2017/.

101 **10,000 "explicitly aggressive":** Demos, "New Demos Study Reveals Scale of Social Media Misogyny," May 26, 2016, http://demos.co.uk/press-release/staggering-scale -of-social-media-misogyny-mapped-in-new-demos-study/.

102 Research conducted by Sonja Starr: Sonja Starr, "Estimating Gender Disparities in Federal Criminal Cases," *Law & Economics Working Papers*, Paper 57, University of Michigan Law School, August 1, 2012, https://repository.law.umich.edu/cgi/view content.cgi?article=1164&context=law_econ_current.

102 forced to register for Selective Service: Gregory Korte, "For a Million U.S. Men, Failing to Register for the Draft Has Serious, Long-Term Consequences," *USA Today*, April 2, 2019, www.usatoday.com/story/news/nation/2019/04/02/failing-register -draft-women-court-consequences-men/3205425002/.

103 men cough up the most cash in tax: Omar Aziz and Norman Gemmell, "Income and Fiscal Incidence by Age and Gender: Some Evidence from New Zealand," *The Review of Income and Wealth*. March 10 2015. Wiley Online Library. https://onlinelibrary .wiley.com/doi/abs/10.1111/roiw.12165.

103 4,492 men died at work in 2015: "Number of Fatal Work Injuries by Employee Status, 2003-15." Bureau of Labor Statistics, 2016.

104 men work longer hours: U.S. Bureau of Labor Statistics, "American Time Use Survey—2014 Results," Time spent working by full- and part-time status, gender, and location in 2014, July 2, 2015, www.bls.gov/opub/ted/2015/time-spent-working -by-full-and-part-time-status-gender-and-location-in-2014.htm.

104 choices made by men and women: U.S. Department of Labor, U.S. Bureau of Labor Statistics, *Highlights of Women's Earnings in 2009*, June 2010, www.bls.gov /opub/reports/womens-earnings/archive/womensearnings_2009.pdf.

104 men chose higher-paying subjects: Anthony P. Carnevale, Nicole Smith, and Artem Gulish, *Women Can't Win: Despite Making Educational Gains and Pursuing High- Wage Majors, Women Still Earn Less than Men*, Georgetown University Center on Education and the Workforce, 2018, https://cew.georgetown.edu/wp-content /uploads/Women_FR_Web.pdf.

104 Just 23 percent of men: Anne Stych, "More Than 40% of Women Leave STEM Jobs after Starting Families," *Chicago Business Journal*, February 26, 2019, www.bizjour nals.com/chicago/news/2019/02/26/40-percent-of-women-leave-stem-jobs-after -kids.html.

104 outearning their male peers: Belinda Luscombe, "Workplace Salaries: At Last, Women on Top," *Time*, September 1, 2010, http://content.time.com/time/business /article/0,8599,2015274,00.html.

105 in free-fall for decades: Federal Bureau of Investigation, "Documents," NICS Firearm Background Checks: November 30, 1998–October 31, 2019, unnumbered chart, www.fbi.gov/file-repository/nics_firearm_checks_-_month_year.pdf /view.

105 the homicide rate fell: Alexia Cooper and Erica L. Smith, *Homicide Trends in the United States, 1980–2008: Annual Rates for 2009 and 2010*, U.S. Department of Justice, Bureau of Justice Statistics, November 2011, www.bjs.gov/content/pub/pdf /htus8008.pdf.

105 gun-related homicides has fallen: Mark J. Perry, "Chart of the Day: More Guns, Less Gun Violence between 1993 and 2013," *AEI* (blog), December 4, 2015, www.aei.org /carpe-diem/chart-of-the-day-more-guns-less-gun-violence-between-1993-and-2013/.

106 **"Some Inconvenient Gun Facts":** Nicholas Kristof, "Some Inconvenient Gun Facts for Liberals," *The New York Times*, January 16, 2016, www.nytimes.com/2016/01/17 /opinion/sunday/some-inconvenient-gun-facts-for-liberals.html.

106 **"changed hands at least once":** U.S. Department of the Treasury, Bureau of Alcohol, Tobacco, and Firearms, "The Youth Crime Gun Interdiction Initiative (YCGII)," *Crime Gun Trace Reports (1999): Highlights of the National Report*, November 2000, www.atf.gov/file/5646/download.

CHAPTER 8: LEARN HOW TO SPOT FAKE NEWS

159 **montage of YouTubers on the front page:** Kevin Roose, "The Making of a YouTube Radical," *The New York Times*, June 9, 2019. www.nytimes.com/images/2019/06/09 /nytfrontpage/scan.pdf?module=inline.

162 **majority of Americans distrust the media:** "Perceived Accuracy and Bias in the Media." Knight Foundation, https://knightfoundation.org/reports/perceived -accuracy-and-bias-in-the-news-media/.

INDEX